MICHELLE OBAMA

MICHELLE OBAMA

A Biography

Alma Halbert Bond

GREENWOOD BIOGRAPHIES

 GREENWOOD

AN IMPRINT OF ABC-CLIO, LLC
Santa Barbara, California • Denver, Colorado • Oxford, England

Library of Congress Cataloging-in-Publication Data

Bond, Alma Halbert.
    Michelle Obama, a biography / Alma Halbert Bond.
        p. cm. — (Greenwood biographies)
    Includes bibliographical references and index.
    ISBN 978-0-313-38104-1 (hardcopy : alk. paper) — ISBN 978-0-313-38105-8
(ebook)   1. Obama, Michelle, 1964– 2. Presidents' spouses—United States—
Biography.   3. African American women—Biography.   4. Chicago (Ill.)—
Biography.   I. Title.
    E909.O24B66   2012
    973.932092—dc23   [B]   2011043426

ISBN: 978-0-313-38104-1
EISBN: 978-0-313-38105-8

16   15   14   13   12   1   2   3   4   5

This book is also available on the World Wide Web as an eBook.
Visit www.abc-clio.com for details.

Greenwood
An Imprint of ABC-CLIO, LLC

ABC-CLIO, LLC
130 Cremona Drive, P.O. Box 1911
Santa Barbara, California 93116-1911

This book is printed on acid-free paper (∞)

Manufactured in the United States of America

This book is dedicated
to my wise and handsome son,
Zane Phillip Bond,
who left us only too soon.
1951–2008

CONTENTS

CONTENTS

SERIES FOREWORD

In response to school and library needs, ABC-CLIO publishes this distinguished series of full-length biographies specifically for student use. Prepared by field experts and professionals, these engaging biographies are tailored for students who need challenging yet accessible biographies. Ideal for school assignments and student research, the length, format, and subject areas are designed to meet educators' requirements and students' interests.

ABC-CLIO offers an extensive selection of biographies spanning all curriculum-related subject areas including social studies, the sciences, literature and the arts, history and politics, and popular culture, covering public figures and famous personalities from all time periods and backgrounds, both historic and contemporary, who have made an impact on American and/or world culture. The subjects of these biographies were chosen based on comprehensive feedback from librarians and educators. Consideration was given to both curriculum relevance and inherent interest. Readers will find a wide array of subject choices from fascinating entertainers like Miley Cyrus and Lady Gaga to inspiring leaders like John F. Kennedy and Nelson Mandela, from the greatest athletes of our time like Michael Jordan and Lance Armstrong, to the most amazing success stories of our day like J. K. Rowling and Oprah.

While the emphasis is on fact, not glorification, the books are meant to be fun to read. Each volume provides in-depth information about the subject's life from birth through childhood, the teen years, and adulthood. A thorough account relates family background and education, traces personal and professional influences, and explores struggles, accomplishments, and contributions. A timeline highlights the most significant life events against an historical perspective. Bibliographies supplement the reference value of each volume.

INTRODUCTION

Michelle Obama is a unique woman, as beautiful on the inside as she is on the outside. Mother, wife, lawyer, career woman, decent human being, her own person in every aspect, she is a superb role model for women of the 21st century. The fact that the president of the United States has Michelle for a wife is a bonus we could not have expected.

Michelle is not a political person, but a woman of whom one can say, "What you see is what you get." She is honest, often brutally so, full of integrity, loving, kind, and an individual who cares deeply about her fellow human beings. She also has a great sense of humor. A few minutes before Barack gave the 2004 Democratic convention keynote address, he told Michelle his stomach was a bit queasy. Michelle looked him straight in the eye and said, "Just don't screw it up, Buddy!" He burst into laughter and was able to relax.

The following quote from her speech at the Women for Obama luncheon on April 18, 2007, is typical of Michelle's philosophy of life and contains in miniature what she feels are the important issues that should guide the president of the United States:

We have spent the last decade talking a good game about family values, but I haven't seen much evidence that we value women or family values.

All of our emotional and financial resources . . . as a country have been totally put into the war. We haven't talked about domestic issues in about 10 years . . . There are no serious conversations about health care or education, or child care, or minimum wage. I mean, these are the basic issues that eat away at the family structure. So you can't just tell a family of four to suck it up and make it work.

That Michelle walks the walk of her philosophy of life is evident in how the Obamas spent Thanksgiving 2008. They took their daughters to work at a food bank on the day before the holiday, saying they wanted to show them the real meaning of Thanksgiving, especially when so many people are struggling and unable to have any dinner at all. They brought Malia and Sasha to join their parents in shaking hands and giving holiday wishes to hundreds of people who had been lined up for hours at the food bank on Chicago's South Side. Barack told reporters he wants his daughters to know how fortunate they are and to make certain they understand the importance of giving back to the community all they have received. Michelle said they want to give their children an understanding of the real meaning of giving and Thanksgiving. The Obamas took their children to work in the cold, when they could easily have gotten aides to hand out the gifts, and taught the girls they are, first and foremost, human beings, not just the kids of a VIP. Let us all learn how to raise our children from the example set by the Obamas.[1]

As first lady, Michelle continues her efforts for community service in a big way. As part of a high-profile effort to spark volunteer work during the summer, Michelle led top members of the Obama administration in fanning out across the country to participate in community service projects.

What better example could there be for the children of America, both black and white? Because Michelle is the kind of person she is—warm, genuine, loving, and caring—she will help heal the split between the races that has long plagued America. Because she is irresistible. Because to know her is to love her.

The importance of a biography of Michelle Obama, first lady of the United States, cannot be overemphasized. The book's subject hopefully will be the second most consequential biography of the times, second only to her husband's. Barack calls his wife "the Boss," which suggests the tremendous influence she has on him. According to biographer Liza Mundy, Michelle is at least as smart as her husband. "She is a better boss than an employee: she likes to be in charge . . . she is forceful and can be intimidating. Her brother says even family members are scared of her,"[2] which, I suspect, includes Barack.

As an example of the enormous effect a first lady can have on a president, Jacqueline Kennedy was very much against nuclear testing. She shared her beliefs with JFK, who formerly was ambivalent about testing. He then proceeded to sign a treaty with Khrushchev banning the testing of atomic bombs. In a similar manner, Michelle Obama privately helps to shape her husband's politics and life. It is also of vital importance that Michelle Obama, the first African American first lady to occupy the White House, has it in her power to change the image of black families and the way black women everywhere regard themselves.

TIMELINE: EVENTS IN THE LIFE OF MICHELLE OBAMA

January 17, 1964	Michelle LaVaughn Robinson born.
1970–1977	Attends Bryn Mawr Elementary School (later, Edward A. Bouchet Elementary School); graduates with honors.
1977–1981	Attends Whitney M. Young Magnet High School.
1981–1985	Matriculates at Princeton University; major in Sociology, minor in African American Studies; awarded Bachelor's Degree in Sociology with cum laude honors.
1985–1988	Attends Harvard Law School; works with Harvard Legal Aid Bureau; earns J.D. degree in 1988.
1988	Joins Sidley & Austin, Chicago law firm (later, Sidley Austin Brown & Wood and then Sidley Austin LLP), focusing on intellectual property rights and marketing.
1989	As a first-year associate at Sidley & Austin, meets Barack Obama, a summer intern.
March 6, 1991	Father, Fraser Robinson, dies, age 55.

1991–1992	Assistant to the Mayor, office of Chicago Mayor Richard M. Daley.
October 3, 1992	Marries Barack Hussein Obama, in Chicago.
1992–1993	Serves as Assistant Commissioner of Planning and Development in the office of Chicago Mayor Richard M. Daley.
1993–1996	Founder and Executive Director of Public Allies Chicago, a branch of an organization devoted to developing young leaders in their communities; the organization later merged into AmeriCorps.
1996–2002	Associate Dean of Student Services, University of Chicago.
July 4, 1998	Daughter Malia born.
June 7, 2001	Daughter Natasha (often called Sasha) born.
2002–2005	Executive Director for Community Affairs, University Chicago Hospitals.
2005–2008	Executive Vice President for Community and External Affairs, University Chicago Hospitals.
2007–2008	Stumps for Barack Obama's presidential election campaign.
August 28, 2008	Delivers keynote address at the Democratic National Convention.
January 20, 2009	Becomes First Lady of the United States on Inauguration Day.

NOTES

1. "Obama Helps at Food Bank," *Associated Press*, November 26, 2008, http://articles.kwch.com/2008-11-26/food-bank_24075866. Page no longer available.

2. Liza Mundy, *Michelle: A Biography* (New York: Simon & Schuster, 2008).

Chapter 1

UP FROM SLAVERY

Can you imagine what the slave Jim Robinson, Michelle Robinson Obama's great-great-grandfather, would have thought if a clairvoyant had told him that some day his great-great-granddaughter would inhabit the White House as first lady of the land? I suspect he would have laughed, as he wearily trudged home from the sprawling rice plantation to the tiny whitewashed wooden cabin where he lived, and muttered, "You mean she will be the first lady's maid?"

Jim Robinson was one of more than 200 slaves that lived and worked on Friendfield Plantation in the small town of Georgetown, South Carolina, in the early 1800s. A map from the era depicts three parallel rows of shacks along Slave Street, a dirt road on the plantation that housed the slave quarters. Several families were jammed into each 19-foot-deep hovel. Additional slaves were packed into attics beneath the roof.[1]

By 1911, the number of remaining hovels had shrunk to 14. Today, only five single structures are left. More than 100 years after the end of the Civil War, the descendants of these slaves could still be found living on this land. The last tenants did not abandon the cabins until the 1960s, and Michelle's great-great-aunt still lives in a whitewashed

bungalow just off the Friendfield lands. Until Michelle visited Georgetown while campaigning for her husband in 2008, she says she had not
known she was descended from a slave.

"It's good to be a part of history in this way," she said in an interview.
"It's us, it's our family, it's that story that's going to play a part in telling a bigger story. It is a process of uncovering the shame, digging out
the pride that is part of that story, so that other folks feel comfortable
about embracing the beauty and the tangled nature of the history of
this country."[2]

Michelle has said that knowing the truth about her family history
has helped her understand her own upbringing, and in a larger sense,
how the legacy of slavery continues to impact the lives of African
Americans to this day. "A lot of times these stories get buried, because
sometimes the pain of them makes it hard to want to remember," she
said. "You've got to be able to acknowledge and understand the past
and move on from it. You have to understand it, and I think a lot of us
just don't have an opportunity to understand it—but it's there."

Much of the wealth of the United States in the first half of the 19th
century was built upon the backs of African Americans. According
to James Oliver Horton, "The slave trade and the products created by
slaves provided the basis for America's wealth as a nation. Such riches
provided some of the capital for the country's industrial revolution
and enabled the United States to project its power into the rest of the
world." Everyone prospered but the slaves.[3]

One of the 14,270,000 slaves was Jim Robinson, of whom we never
would have heard had he not been the great-great-grandfather of Michelle Obama. It is not known how or when he came to Friendfield,
but census records reveal that his parents were born in South Carolina.
Jim, who was born about 1850, lived in one of the shacks and worked in
the riverfront rice fields as a slave until the Civil War. He was tall and
slender, as his great-great-granddaughter would be more than a century
later. He was also hardworking and a devoted family man, values Michelle would share. After Lincoln freed the slaves, Robinson, like many
of his former countrymen, continued to inhabit the old slave quarters
with his wife, Louiser, and their children, and worked as a sharecropper.

His son Fraser, Michelle's great-grandfather, was born in 1884. Unable to read or write, Jim was destined to be the last illiterate member

of Michelle Obama's family. The date of his death is not known, but historians believe he was buried in an unmarked grave in the dilapidated African American slave cemetery that overlooks the rice fields. Michelle recently was invited to view the graveyard.

If Michelle's great-great-grandfather would have been astounded to learn that his great-great-granddaughter was living in the White House, not as a maid, but as the first lady, he would not have been alone in his reaction. When Obama won the election, people shouted, "Can you believe it? I never thought I'd live to see an African American elected president of the United States!" as they danced in the street.

Barack Obama has called his wife "the most quintessentially American woman I know," and indeed, Michelle Obama and her family's history seems to embody the American dream. The fact that the Robinsons were involved in so many formative aspects of the African American experience makes her position as America's first lady all the more impressive. Rep. James E. Clyburn (D) of South Carolina, whose district includes part of Georgetown County, has commented on the significance that the first lady is descended from slaves: "It would allow us an opportunity to get beyond some of our preconceived notions, some of our prejudices." Clyburn believes her role is equally, if not more, important than her husband's.

Francis Withers, Jim Robinson's master, was the original owner of Friendfield Plantation. Friendfield had more than 500 acres of rice fields, and its production of Carolina Gold made it one of the most successful plantations in the region. In comparison to the average slave owner of his day, Withers treated his slaves well and even provided for their care in his will, leaving instructions that his slaves were to be treated with "great kindness and be fed and clothed." Withers also left extra money to induce his relatives to keep the "Friendfield gang of slaves" together and not break up families, as many slave owners did.[4] His kindness allowed the family of Michelle Obama's great-great-grandfather to stay together. If it hadn't been for Withers's compassion, Michelle Obama might not exist today.

Jim Robinson's children included Fraser Robinson, Michelle Obama's great-grandfather, who was born in 1884. As a child, he was employed as a houseboy with the family of Francis Nesmith, the son of an overseer at another plantation. Nesmith liked the child so much he treated him as one of his own. Apparently, Michelle's charisma has been handed down to her through her genes, as the Robinson charm goes way back in time. The boy was illiterate as an adolescent but, demonstrating the family's innate intelligence, taught himself to read and write by the time he had his own children. As a young man, Fraser found employment as a lumber-mill laborer, newspaper salesman, and shoemaker, despite the fact that his left arm had been amputated as a result of a boyhood injury in which a sapling fell on him, causing a compound fracture that became septic.

"It makes more sense to me," Michelle has said. "If the patriarch in our lineage was one-armed Fraser, a shoemaker with one arm, an entrepreneur, someone who was able to own property, and with sheer effort and determination was able to build a life in this town—that must have been the messages that my grandfather got."[5] Her ancestors' attitude of "I'm going to do it, whatever the cost" lives on in Michelle Obama today.

Fraser Robinson married a woman named Rose Ella Cohen, whose last name suggests that Jewish blood flows in Michelle's veins. This would mean that, for the first time in history, at least in known records, there may be Jewish blood in the White House. In fact, Michelle Obama's cousin is Rabbi Capers Funnye, chief rabbi of the Beth Shalom B'nai Zaken Ethiopian Hebrew Congregation, a predominantly black Chicago synagogue. Funnye's mother, Verdelle Robinson Funnye, was Fraser Robinson's daughter, and the sister of Michelle's grandfather, Fraser Jr.[6]

Fraser was an intelligent man who wanted his children to be well-read. After reading the *Palmetto Leader and Grit*, a popular black newspaper, he would bring home extra copies for his family. According to Margretta Dunmore Knox, a resident of Georgetown who knew the Robinson family from church, Fraser would make his children read the newspapers he brought home.[7]

Fraser Jr., Robinson's eldest son and grandfather of Michelle Obama, was born in 1912 and was the first member of the Robinson family to graduate from high school. He was a top student as well as a fine orator. It is conceivable that Michelle inherited her grandfather's oratorical skills, along with his intelligence.[8]

At that time, Georgetown, a coastal town about an hour's drive north of Charleston, was split along racial lines. Out of the need to earn a living, as well as escape the escalating prejudice, Fraser Robinson, Jr., became part of the Great Migration. Some six million African Americans, fed by the Industrial Revolution, poured out of the Jim Crow South into the great Northern cities and the West. In search of work, Fraser left his family for 14 years, and as a result, his family was forced to resort to welfare in the interim. Fraser Jr., made his way to Chicago, where work was available in the mills, meat-packing plants, and slaughterhouses. Along with the hordes of other African Americans arriving in Chicago, Fraser Jr., found himself herded into a small strip of land south of the heart of the city. Blacks were not permitted to live outside that area, and they disregarded the restrictions even momentarily at great cost, sometimes paying with their lives.

Chicago in the 1960s was one of the most segregated cities in the United States. Eventually, 500,000 African Americans would move to Chicago from the South, greatly expanding the black population. Certain influential residents, backed by politicians and real estate agents, succeeded in keeping the blacks confined to their overcrowded neighborhoods and schools, going so far as to relocate the Dan Ryan expressway to block off the black ghetto. Their efforts, backed by politicians, real estate agents, and residents, were successful for a very long time. The rampant discrimination in housing persisted until six months after the birth of Michelle, when the 1964 Civil Rights Act was passed by President Lyndon Johnson. The act prohibited discrimination in government and public housing. Thus, new residential possibilities were created for families like the Robinsons, who, by the time Michelle was a child, were able to move into a neighborhood formerly occupied only by whites.

The South remained even more segregated and racist. The Ku Klux Klan lynched thousands of black people. The government and police did little to stop them—indeed, certain uniformed officers even joined the lynchers. Growing up black in Georgetown meant constant humiliation to people like the Robinsons, as water fountains were marked "Coloreds" or "Whites" and rest rooms were reserved "For Whites Only." African Americans were permitted to sit only in the back of buses, regardless of whether or not seats were available anywhere else. Michelle's grandfather "was a very proud man, who was proud of his lineage," she has said, but he was not altogether happy about living in Chicago. After retiring, the Robinsons returned to Georgetown and joined the oldest black church in the city, AME Bethel Church, which had been founded by freed slaves in 1865, where the Robinson family had worshiped since the turn of the century. The couple sang in the choir and established a large coterie of friends.

Although Michelle Obama has visited Georgetown many times and recalls passing by the Friendfield gate as a child, her family never discussed the ancestors that had once been slaves on that land.[9]

The third Fraser Robinson, born in Chicago in 1935, and his wife, Marian, also a Chicago native, whom we know as Michelle's parents, lived on the South Side of Chicago while their children were growing up.

Genealogical researcher Megan Smolenyak, in 2009, traced Marian Shields Robinson's ancestry to Melvinia, a South Carolina slave bequeathed as a child to the wife of Henry Shields, a Georgia farmer. As a teenager, Melvinia, who gave all four of her children the name Shields after emancipation, gave birth to a son by an unknown white father. Her son, Dolphus T. Shields, was Marian Shields's great-great-grandfather.[10]

It seems that in order to keep Michelle's and Craig's self-images high, the senior Robinsons, who were well aware of Fraser's slave ancestry, if not Marian's, kept the knowledge from their children.

Michelle returned to the Georgetown church while campaigning in the South Carolina presidential primary for her husband. There, she addressed a wall-to-wall audience that included 31 of her relatives who were descendants of Jim Robinson.[11] Michelle Robinson Obama, great-great-granddaughter of a slave, had come home in triumph, the stuff of which dreams are made.

NOTES

1. Dahleen Glanton and Stacy St. Clair, "Michelle Obama's Family Tree Has Roots in a Carolina Slave Plantation," *Chicago Tribune*, December 1, 2008, http://www.chicagotribune.com/news/local/chi-obama-slavery-01-dec01,0,485324.story?page=1.

2. Shailagh Murray, "A Family Tree Rooted in American Soil," *Washington Post*, October 2, 2008, http://www.washingtonpost.com/wp-dyn/content/article/2008/10/01/AR2008100103169.html?sid=ST2008100103245&s_pos=.

3. James Oliver Horton and Lois E. Horton, *Slavery and the Making of America* (New York: Oxford University Press, 2005), 7.

4. Glanton and St. Clair, "Michelle Obama's Family Tree Has Roots in a Carolina Slave Plantation."

5. Murray, "A Family Tree Rooted in American Soil."

6. Anthony Weiss, "Michelle Obama Has a Rabbi in Her Family," *Jewish Daily Forward*, September 2, 2008; Liza Mundy, *Michelle, A Biography* (New York: Simon & Schuster, 2008).

7. Glanton and St. Clair, "Michelle Obama's Family Tree Has Roots in a Carolina Slave Plantation."

8. Jodi Kantor, "Nation's Many Faces in Extended First Family," *New York Times*, January 26, 2009.

9. Murray, "A Family Tree Rooted in American Soil."

10. Jodi Kantor and Rachel L. Swarns, "In First Lady's Roots, a Complex Path from Slavery," *New York Times*, October 7, 2009.

11. Glanton and St. Clair, "Michelle Obama's Family Tree Has Roots in a Carolina Slave Plantation."

Chapter 2

MARIAN ROBINSON, MICHELLE'S MOTHER

She is a tall, stately, attractive, intelligent, elegantly dressed black woman with a terrific sense of humor. No, I am not describing Michelle Obama, but her mother, Marian Robinson. Were they the same age, they might easily be mistaken for each other. In a photo of the Fraser Robinson family taken when the children were toddlers, I had to check to make sure the woman pictured was Marian and not Michelle.

Marian L. Shields was born in 1937 on the South Side of Chicago, where she met Fraser Robinson. They married in 1960. Both had grown up in the same neighborhood, and decided to raise their own family there. Two years later, Craig was born, followed, on January 17, 1964, by Michelle LaVaughn.

The South Side is a black island in a largely white city. It isn't one neighborhood, like New York City's Harlem, for example, but a collection of smaller neighborhoods scattered over 60 percent of the city. The sprawling South Side is arguably the country's largest black enclave.

Life was not easy for the Robinsons, living in an underprivileged area with very little money, but it created values in Marian she was able to pass on to her children. Michelle learned from her mother that life was going to be hard, but no matter what it takes, you just had to do the job and do it well.

"If we had a chore, we had to do it right," Michelle's brother, Craig Robinson, the men's basketball coach at Oregon State University, has said.[1] Michelle learned the lesson very well. Whatever she touches, whether it be school, the law, marriage, being a mother, or a style setter, she does it right.

Marian worked as a secretary at Spiegel catalog until Craig was born, when she left her job to be a full-time mother. While Michelle was growing up, the Robinsons rented a one-bedroom apartment in a brick bungalow from her great aunt, who lived on the ground floor. Marian and Fraser occupied the only bedroom of the apartment and partitioned the 16 × 18 foot living room into three parts: a bedroom for Michelle, one for Craig, and a third section reserved for studying.[2]

"It was tight, but adequate," Craig Robinson said.[3] "Come to think of it, it was very tight. But it's funny, when you're in a situation, it's seems fine, but when you look back you wonder how you did it."[4]

Although the space indeed was cramped for the tall occupants (Michelle is 5 foot 11 inches and Craig 6 foot 6 inches tall), its division dramatically illustrates what was important to the parents, who sacrificed their living room to give the children a room of their own and a special place to study. Marian lives there still, when she is not at the White House. She occupies the whole house now, in the same part of town where she and her husband were born. Despite the fact that the urban area was full of problems, the Robinsons were determined to keep their children safe from the pull of the unhealthy environment, and to teach them to work to the best of their ability, to reach for the sky, and to never, never give up.

We don't know whether Marian had read the works of Freud, but if she didn't, she didn't need to. The most important lesson she taught her children was how enormously significant parents are in a child's development. When they were small, Michelle and Craig were expected to join their parents for a family dinner every night. No excuses were acceptable. It was an important Robinson ritual, where the daily experiences of the family members, current events, and individual problems were discussed, and in the latter case, hopefully, resolved. It was probably at the family dinner table that Michelle learned her debating skills, which were to serve her well as a lawyer and, indeed, on the campaign trail for Barack.

That this skill was acquired early and practiced voraciously is indicated in a small ad the senior Robinsons took out in the Princeton Year Book when Michelle graduated. The ad said, "We knew you would do this fifteen years ago when we could never make you shut up."

The children were expected to do their chores. They alternated washing the dishes, while Michelle's job every Saturday was to clean the bathroom. The future first lady had to scrub the sink, mop the floor, and clean the toilet. Barack later described the Robinsons as similar to the family in *Leave It to Beaver,* a well-functioning brood with whom the parents got along well, and they loved and nurtured their children who, nevertheless, were expected to work hard and be successful. They all went to church. Michelle was a Brownie and a Girl Scout. Both children took piano lessons and drama classes and were taken to museums and the Art Institute.[5]

Michelle grew up with a grandmother and an aunt, who escorted her to places when her mother couldn't. It was an ideal family scene, marred only by the absence of a dog. Marian refused to have a dog mess up her spotless house. This void in Michelle's life was not to be filled until she became the first lady.

Marian Robinson was loving but tough-minded. Michelle and Craig were permitted to watch only a single hour of television a night, and they were encouraged to devote their time to reading and mind-enhancing games such as chess. Although neither parent had attended college, they were greatly aware of the importance of education. In addition to making sure the children attended school regularly, Marian taught them at home, bringing math and reading workbooks from school so that they were always ahead of their classmates. They got up at 4:30 every morning to attend lessons with the loving taskmaster, who insisted on discipline and chores to teach them responsibility. Not surprisingly, both children learned to read by the age of four, and skipped the second grade. Although neither parent had gone to college, Marian and Fraser also had skipped a grade in grammar school, suggesting that they had a natural intelligence that was inherited by their children.

Marian believed that learning to think and ask questions was even more important than mastering reading and writing. She told Lauren

Collins in an interview for the *New Yorker* that she had taught her children to respect their teachers but not to fear asking them questions. "Don't even allow *us* to just say anything to you," she said. "Ask us why."[6] She said she always encouraged her children to express what was on their minds, even though it often is difficult to do so, and not to let people stop them from telling the truth.

"My parents told us time and time again," Michelle said.[7] "Don't tell us what you can't do. And don't worry what can go wrong."[8] Michelle has followed their advice ever since. With this background, it is not surprising that Michelle always speaks candidly, even when it gets her into trouble, and has taught her children to do the same. Marian follows her own advice and rarely refrains from coming out with what is on her mind. Perhaps her teachings will seep down to the country as a whole and usher in a refreshing new era of truth and honesty.

Although Marian Robinson was a very conscientious mother, with strict rules and discipline, she is a very different kind of a grandmother. She is outspoken about the fact that she disagrees with her daughter on child rearing. "She has them so, I don't know, like little soldiers," Marian said, forgetting she had the same standards when raising Michelle and Craig. Marian thinks their rules of one hour daily of TV and an 8:30 bedtime are much too strict. "That's ridiculous!" she has said. "An hour of TV is just not enough!"[9] She adores Malia and Sasha and says she likes to spoil them.

When Michelle Obama was campaigning for her husband, Marian's day was fully scheduled: she slept over at the Obama house, woke the girls in the morning, and made them breakfast according to the rigid restrictions set by Michelle, who allows them to eat only organic and natural foods. Marian packed their lunches, checked that their hair was combed properly, and chauffeured them to school. Most days, after school, she drove the girls to piano or dance lessons, gymnastics, tennis, or soccer. After their lessons, she fixed dinner (nutritional requirements followed, of course), checked their homework, against her will restricted their TV watching to one hour a day, according to the dictates of their mother, and then tucked them into bed. She loves being around her granddaughters and refuses to hire a babysitter. In their family there are so many aunts, cousins, and uncles pining to be with the children, she believes there is no reason to hire a sitter. Family is better is her motto.

Like her famous daughter, Marian has a good sense of humor, and is able to laugh at herself. She has said, "The whole time I raised Craig and Michelle, I was telling them I raised my own kids, so don't expect me to raise any kids of yours!" Then she added with a laugh, "and just look at what I'm doing now!" But this loving grandmother cannot imagine allowing anyone else to do it. "If someone besides their mother has to take care of them," she said, "it better be me."[10]

When the girls are at Marian Robinson's house, things are very different. "I give them candy and let them stay up late. In my house, they can watch TV as long as they want to, and we play games late into the night," Robinson said. "I do everything that grandmothers do that they're not supposed to." No wonder Malia and Sasha adore their grandmother!

Marian also objects to the natural food Michelle serves the children: "That's not my thing. If you are going to have fried chicken, have fried chicken!" Marian Robinson should know: she makes the best fried chicken in the world. Crumbling Ritz crackers in the batter, she bathes the pieces of chicken in ice water before she fries them, saying it makes them crispier, and adds lots of salt and oil.[11] The children love it.

Marian went on to lecture Michelle that *she* was fed good-tasting food when she was growing up, and it is too late for her (Marian) to change.

Barack doesn't argue with her. "I don't tell my mother-in-law what to do. I'm not stupid—that's why I got elected president, man."[12]

In spite of their minor differences, Michelle is bringing up her daughters in much the same way as she was raised. "Mom, what are you rolling your eyes at? You made us do the same thing," Michelle told her mother, according to Marian in her March 2008 interview with Scott Helman of the *Boston Globe*. "I don't remember being that bad," she said. "It seems like she's just going overboard."[13]

Mrs. Robinson needn't feel defensive about the fact that she and her daughter have many of the same ideas about raising children. Michelle's supremely confident manner with Malia and Sasha may be due, in part, to the fact that she shares her mother's beliefs about child rearing. My doctoral dissertation at Columbia University, "Grandmothers' Attitudes and Mothers' Concerns," found results that indicate that mothers who have much the same attitudes toward child rearing as their own mothers are far less anxious in raising their children than female parents whose philosophies of child rearing differ from those held by their mothers. Although mothers interviewed for the project on the whole tended to be more permissive than grandmothers, the study found that the greater the difference between the attitudes of mother and grandmother, the greater the number of concerns in the mother. Attitudes tested include suppressive attitude to others, rejection of homemaking, demand for striving, and harsh punitive control—all of which Marian and Michelle seem to agree upon.[14]

A favorite story of Marian's concerns an elementary schoolteacher of Michelle's who complained that she had a terrible temper. Marian told the teacher, "Yeah, she's got a temper. But we decided to keep her anyway."[15]

Marian Robinson is not exactly a spendthrift. Years after Michelle moved away from the small brick house in Westburn, Marian has not changed a thing about the bedroom. Mrs. Obama has teased her about getting a new bed, but admits that her children love the old-fashioned furnishings.

It is a tidy little house in a predominantly black working-class neighborhood, secure and affordable. Marian sent her children to the grammar school down the block. The South Shore Methodist Church, where the family worshipped, was just across the street. Marian Robinson loved the house then and she loves it still.

In that home, she brought up two future Ivy League students, took care of her disabled husband, who died in 1991, and then lived happily alone as a widow for almost 20 years. She parked her car on the street and shoveled snow from the pavement herself. When it was too cold to go outside, Marian played the piano or watched TV, surrounded by photographs of four generations of her family. On warmer days, she sat on the sun porch reading the newspaper and doing the crossword puzzles. She was happy in the home where she had come as a bride and raised her children, and never expected to leave it. She tells friends that her move to Washington probably is temporary. She expects she will stay there only as long as she is needed, and then return to her beloved little home.

Marian's life suited her very well. Grounded in routine, almost all her activities revolved around family. Until 2008, when she retired from her job as an assistant in the trust department of a downtown bank, she was part of a car pool with her sister, Grace Hale, who lives around the corner. On Thursdays, she took a yoga class taught by her brother Steve Shields. On Saturday mornings, she had her hair done at a downtown hair salon and then drove to River Oaks Mall with Grace. There the sisters treated themselves to lunch at Bennigan's or Red Lobster. On the drive home, they stopped to do their weekly grocery shopping. Marian's life was predictable, unvarying, and pleasant. Until Barack Obama ran for president.

Marian doesn't live much differently than her own mother. She was the child of a painter and a full-time mother with seven children, who lived in a small house on the South Side. Five of Marian's siblings are still alive and live within 15 miles of each other. The family is very close and meet on holidays and for impromptu meals. When Michelle and Barack Obama married, the family took him in as one of their own.

Marian Robinson is a loving but firm matriarch who is as integral to the Obama family as Michelle or Barack. She retired in order to care for her granddaughters while their parents were on the campaign trail.[16] From the looks of the girls, being supervised by their grandmother has not damaged them one bit.

Marian's pleasant room in the White House is on the third floor, just one level above the Obamas. In it are an inviting four-poster bed and a TV set. There is a large walk-in closet, and a small sitting area for favored guests. What Marian likes best about her room is that Malia's and Sasha's playroom is just down the hall, and she can drop in on them whenever she pleases. A solarium is nearby, where she can relax on a deep, soft sofa or look out the large bay windows at the magnificent Washington Monument and a panoramic view of the city. Despite the fact that she is surrounded by beauty and luxury, the loving mother and grandmother still yearns at times for her comfortable life in Chicago, but she is committed to making the president and her daughter feel at home in Washington.

As if Barack Obama hasn't already pulled off enough firsts, he insists that he wants his mother-in-law to live in the White House as long as the Obamas do. It is fun to picture Michelle Obama's mother lounging around the stately mansion and scolding the president for running the country so badly. But should anyone dare to agree, Mrs. Robinson will be sure to let them have it, too.

Marian Robinson and her daughter Michelle at the Democratic National Convention in Denver, August 26, 2008. (AP Photo/Ted S. Warren, File.)

Michelle agrees with her husband's feelings about his mother-in-law. At the Democratic National Convention in 2008, Michelle said, "My mother's love has always been the sustaining force for our family. One of my greatest joys is seeing her integrity, her compassion, and her intelligence reflected in my daughters." At the beginning of Barack's run for the presidency, Mrs. Robinson opposed his plans. Like all the rest of the country, she was worried about his safety, should he be elected president. Marian was a young woman in the 1960s, and the horror of President John F. Kennedy's assassination is permanently etched in her mind, and she believes that many bigoted people would be happy to see a black president murdered. But, she thought Barack would make a great president and—thanks in part to a lecture from her son, Craig—became reconciled to the idea of her son-in-law being president.

Being who she is, Mrs. Robinson plays a critical role during the Obama presidency in her effort to keep her granddaughters' lives as normal as possible. However, she has always valued her independence. She eschewed her parents' desires for her to become a teacher and, instead, made her career as a secretary. Despite the fact that people told her she was "too old to be running around like a teenager," she ran the 50-and 100-yard dashes in the Illinois senior games.[17] And she often teases her daughter and the president about their household rules for Sasha and Malia.

Mrs. Robinson is deeply rooted in Chicago and the small brick bungalow where she came as a bride and brought up her children. She is able to live very comfortably on the pension she receives from her late husband's job. Barack doubted that she would agree to relocate to Washington. After he was elected president, Obama said on 60 Minutes that he very much wanted her to live with them. "She's just been an unbelievable support for all of us during this process," he said. "But she likes her own space. She doesn't like a lot of fuss around her. And, like it or not, there's some fuss in the White House. But we hope that she comes."[18] The White House is very different from the black working-class neighborhood on Chicago's South Side where Mrs. Robinson and her late husband, Fraser Robinson, brought up their son and daughter. And Marian is not sure yet she prefers the former to the latter. "I've never lived outside of Chicago, so I don't know," Mrs. Robinson said, as she was considering moving into the White House. "The White House reminds me of a museum," she told a magazine interviewer. "How do you sleep in a museum? . . . In the end, I'll do whatever Michelle needs me to do," she said. "I'll be mad, but I'll do it."[19]

Senior advocates have praised Marian, saying that her move to the White House demonstrates that living with grown children does not necessarily mean giving up one's independence. "She is the kind of role model you want," according to AARP spokeswoman Nancy Thompson. "She's an active retiree with her own life."[20]

"The Obama children are going to be living in a very confusing, pressure-ridden environment, and to have [her] to call upon for that unconditional love . . . is a wonderful thing," said Paul Arfin, president of Intergenerational Strategies. "It's also a wonderful opportunity to demonstrate to the nation how a grandparent can play a role like this."[21] She isn't the first mother-in-law to live in the White House. Dwight D. Eisenhower shared his living quarters with Mamie's mother, Elvira Doud, although it can be surmised that Eisenhower felt quite differently from Barack about his mother-in-law sharing his living quarters. But then Marian is very different from Elvira Doud. Bess Truman's mother, Madge Gates Wallace, was another curmudgeon who lived in the White House. She considered her son-in-law, President Harry S. Truman, to be from a lower social class and said she knew "dozens of men better qualified" to preside over the country.[22]

Both Michelle and Barack are very grateful to Marian Robinson and doubt they could have made the transition without her.

"I am standing here breathing in and out with any level of calm because my 70-year-old [mother] is home with my girls," Michelle told voters in Chillicothe, Ohio, on one of the dozens of campaign trips she made.[23]

Indeed, it is hardly clear Barack Obama would be president, or that his wife would have let him, were his mother-in-law not in the picture. "I'm not sure we could do it," he said. "I'm not sure Michelle would have felt comfortable with it, and I probably would have agreed with her." The support Marian provides, he added, has helped the family survive his transition to national politics.

"One of the best decisions we made when I was elected to the Senate was that we wouldn't move from Chicago. A big reason for that was that Marian lived ten minutes away," he continued. "She loves nothing more than to spend time with her grandkids."[24]

Disagreements over fried food aside, observers predict a smooth relationship between the Obamas and Marian in the White House. Indeed, the photo of Obama and his mother-in-law sitting side by side on a couch and holding hands as they watched election-night returns is very moving. Lucky mother-in-law! Lucky son-in-law! We should all be so blessed.

NOTES

1. Interview with Craig Robinson, *New York Times,* 2007, quoted in Rachel L. Swarns, "Family Mainstay to Move In to White House," *New York Times,* January 9, 2009, http://www.nytimes.com/2009/01/10/us/politics/10marian.html.

2. Ibid.

3. Ibid.

4. Ibid.

5. David Bergen Brophy, *Michelle Obama: Meet the First Lady* (New York: HarperCollins, 2009), 14.

6. Lauren Collins, "The Other Obama," *New Yorker*, March 10, 2008, http://www.newyorker.com/reporting/2008/03/10/080310fa_fact_collins?currentPage=all.

7. Scott Helman, "Holding Down the Obama Family Fort, 'Grandma' Makes the Race Possible," *Boston Globe*, March 30, 2008.

8. Ibid.

9. Ibid.

10. Ibid.

11. Ibid.

12. President-elect Barack Obama, interview with Steve Kroft, *60 Minutes* (November 16, 2008).

13. Helman, "Holding Down the Obama Family Fort, 'Grandma' Makes the Race Possible."

14. Alma H. Bond, "Grandmothers' Attitudes and Mothers' Concerns" (unpublished thesis, Columbia University, 1961).

15. Swarns, "Family Mainstay to Move In to White House."

16. Ibid.

17. Ibid.

18. Kroft, *60 Minutes*.

19. Sandra Sobieraj Westfall, "Five Things to Know about Grandma-in-Chief Marian Robinson," *People*, January 20, 2009.

20. Nancy Thompson, quoted in Stacy St. Clair, "Barack Obama's Mother-in-Law Will Move to White House for Trial Visit," *Chicago Tribune*, January 12, 2009, http://articles.chicagotribune.com/2009-01-12/news/0901110543_1_mother-in-law-obama-transition-team-michelle-obama.

21. Paul Arfin, quoted in Carol Polsky, "Families Applaud Obama's Mother-in-Law Moving into White House to Help Care for Kids," *Newsday*, January 25, 2009.

22. Carl Sferrazza Anthony, quoted in Beth Teitell, "Granny Diplomacy; When a Mother-in-Law Moves In, It's an Adjustment for Everyone (Even a President)," *Boston Globe*, December 30, 2008.

23. Helman, "Holding Down the Obama Family Fort, 'Grandma' Makes the Race Possible."

24. Ibid.

Chapter 3

FRASER ROBINSON III, MICHELLE'S FATHER

Fraser Robinson III might have been mistaken for a white-collar worker, thanks to his clothing and demeanor, but he was actually a blue-collar man. He was a nice looking person with a kind face, who sported a long, thin mustache extending to his lower lip and horn-rimmed glasses. Shorter than his wife, he was already balding in his early 30s.

More important, Fraser Robinson III was a superb father. If one didn't hear words of praise describing him over and over again from his wife, Marian; Michelle; her brother, Craig; and Barack Obama himself, it would be difficult to believe that any parent could be such a paragon. But, when one considers the way both his children turned out, the idea becomes more feasible.

Fraser Robinson III was very influenced by his own father's frugality, which had a significant bearing on the lives of his children. Fraser Robinson Jr., Michelle Obama's grandfather, was a very frugal man. Terrified of being in debt, he would not allow his oldest son, the third Fraser Robinson, to borrow the money he needed for his college tuition. Although Fraser III was a highly intelligent man, he had to drop out of college after only one year. He went on to work in a city boiler room for the rest of his life. As a result, he avoided duplicating his father's behavior at any cost, making sure he raised the money to send Michelle and Craig to Princeton.

Many generations of Robinsons had taught their children that education is the only way for them to succeed in a racist society. Craig Robinson said his mother taught him, "When you acquire knowledge, you acquire something no one could take away from you."[1] According to census records, each generation of Robinsons became more educated than the last, culminating in Michelle's and Craig's Ivy League schooling.

During Michelle's youth, Chicago was almost completely segregated under Richard J. Daley, the Democratic mayor, whose policies and programs created rigid racial barriers and enforced unmitigated discrimination. Daley and his associates used public housing, patronage, and school board officials to keep Chicago segregated, while maintaining the support of black voters. For example, his construction of what is now called the Eisenhower Expressway sliced the tough West Side neighborhood of Lawndale in two "and essentially destroyed it."[2]

Daley managed to do his dirty work with a political structure in which a few African Americans were rewarded with jobs for helping to keep other blacks oppressed. According to Pamela Geller in the New American Independent, Michelle Obama's father was one of the African Americans so rewarded. Robinson was an organizer for Chicago's Democratic Party. As a reward for his work with the party, he was hired as an engineer with the city's water department. Hired as a caretaker in the city's water plant, he worked swing shifts in which he tended the boilers at a water filtration plant. When he first began the job, he did menial work, such as cleaning, washing floors, and general janitorial jobs. But as he became more valued, he was promoted to do administrative work. First serving as a volunteer for the Democratic Party, he eventually was advanced to volunteer precinct captain. As such, he became a formidable neighborhood leader, going from door to door promoting the Democratic candidates running for election in the district, handing out information about the party, and talking with the constituents. The most important aspect of Fraser's job was to make sure people got to the polls to vote for machine-supported candidates.

In those times of great racial prejudice, a job with the city was especially valuable to an African American, because it provided protection from the overt racism of the marketplace. By the end of his career, before overtime, Fraser Robinson was earning more than $40,000 a year.[3] He also was able to work as many overtime hours as he wished, at double the hourly wage, bringing his salary up to $60,000 a year. This was more than that earned by experienced Chicago teachers. Because his income was relatively good, his wife Marian was able to stay at home with the children as a full-time mother, an option rarely available to black women. Perhaps most important of all to Robinson was the fact that only by working with the machine could he afford to educate his children.

We cannot be certain whether or not Fraser Robinson knew that he was helping to enforce segregation in the city of Chicago when he inveigled constituents to vote for corrupt politicians. But, if he had refused to go along with the machine, he most certainly would have been fired. In the opinion of the author, he could not afford the luxury of speaking the truth. As he was not a complainer, it is unlikely that the young Michelle and Craig understood the part their father played in working to perpetuate the Daley political machine in Chicago. If they had, they may well have thought of it as simply another sacrifice Robinson had to make to keep his beloved family alive and well.

Lee Cary of the *American Thinker* states his opinion about Barack Obama's relationship to the machine, which is quite opposite from the one held by the Robinson family. Cary believes Barack Obama learned power politics from the Daleys. According to Cary, "Old guard Beltway politicos marvel at Obama's skill at concentrating power. He learned it from the Daley's . . . Obama is establishing his own parallel bureaucracy answerable only to him. Hence the platoon of czars. Daily, many Cabinet positions are becoming merely ceremonial."[4]

At Davis Miner Barnhill & Galland, Allison Davis was Barack Obama's mentor in the intricacies of subsidized housing. Obama, Cary continues, learned a lot from Davis. He also was taught a great deal by Michelle Robinson, who once worked in the office of the mayor. (*Et tu*, Michelle? But then, she did quit the job!) Her boss there was Valerie Jarrett, later a senior advisor in the White House. Cary believes it is necessary to view the current presidency through the Office of the Mayor of Chicago, if we want to understand the way the president functions today. Could be. I don't like to think so, but could be.

Craig Robinson's picture of Obama's relationship to the machine is very different from Cary's. "We as a family were extremely cynical about politics and politicians."[5] That didn't change until Barack Obama, who stood in opposition to Daley and aimed to break up the machine, came into the picture.

Michelle speaks poignantly about the importance of Fraser's job. He was diagnosed with multiple sclerosis (MS) in his early 30s. Despite the pain and inconvenience of remastering even simple tasks like buttoning his shirts, Fraser never gave up working. Michelle said her father was "a man who didn't complain, was never late, never expressed any level of doubt about his situation in life, and taught us that we could dream of anything." Fraser Robinson kept his optimistic attitude even though he had given up his own hopes and dreams so his children could achieve theirs. He taught Michelle and Craig that they could have anything they wanted in life, as long as they worked hard enough for it.

"That's the voice in my head that keeps me whole and grounded and keeps me the girl from the South Side of Chicago," Michelle said of her father, "no matter how many cameras are in the room, how many autographs people want, how big we get."[6]

Craig Robinson's feelings about his father were equally glowing. He said Fraser was smart, hardworking, raised two intelligent kids, provided a great family atmosphere, and did it all on a laborer's salary. "My father was not college-educated," Craig said, "but was 'full of integrity,' the 'gold standard' of husbands, and 'a hardworking man' who raised two kids when he had multiple sclerosis."[7] Fraser demonstrated his fine character even as a young man, when he unselfishly dropped out of college in order to send his younger brother to school.

Fraser encouraged his son to attend Princeton University, despite the fact that Craig had been offered substantial scholarships at other universities. "If you pick a school based on what I have to pay," he told Craig, "I'll be very disappointed."[8] He and Marian paid for their son's education with money from an insurance policy and a credit card.

Craig says, "My father's decision changed my whole life. It changed all of our lives. If I hadn't gone to Princeton, my sister probably wouldn't

Craig Robinson shares a moment with sister Michelle at the Democratic National Convention, August 26, 2008. (AP Photo/Ted S. Warren.)

have gone to Princeton and she never would've met Barack and none of this would've happened. All because of my father."[9]

Fraser Robinson died in 1991. According to both his children, their father never raised his voice to them, saying only "I'm disappointed" when they misbehaved. He never used corporal punishment on them, either, although Marian Robinson had been known to do so.

"You never wanted to disappoint him," Michelle told author Richard Wolffe. "We would be bawling."[10]

The great tragedy of the family was that Fraser Robinson was stuck down with MS at 30, the usual age for the onset of the disease. MS is a very common neurological disorder, the cause or causes of which are as yet unknown. Fortunately for Michelle and Craig, it is not passed genetically. A disease of the central nervous system, impulses that carry messages from the brain and spinal cord are interrupted and cause reduced or loss of bodily functions. The disease progresses inexorably toward the final stage of death.[11]

Michelle was deeply moved by her father's stoicism about his illness and thought of him as an unsung hero. Even though he must have been in agony at times, he never showed evidence of it. One of the distressing symptoms caused by the illness is extreme fatigue, which gets worse in the afternoon, the very time Fraser was hard at work. As one MS patient said, "I thought they were kidding when they said I would get fatigued! I thought I already knew fatigued!"[12] Only his extreme courage and determination to keep going for the sake of his family kept Fraser functioning through the exhaustion brought on by the disease.

To add to Fraser's problems, heat can be devastating for someone with MS, when a rise in temperature makes the afflicted person feel miserable. Keeping cool with air-conditioning is helpful for people with MS. But boiler rooms, where Fraser worked, are often insufferably hot and not noted for their air-conditioning, particularly in times past. We can picture Fraser hobbling around on two canes and dripping with sweat, as he went about his business. One of the reasons he found it so hard to walk may have been that he, like many victims of MS, suffered from a disability called foot drop, in which it is difficult to lift the front part of the foot. Walking or driving with foot drop is extremely difficult. It occurs because the message from the brain to lift the foot doesn't make it all the way down. The foot itself is just fine; it is the orders to move it that are lacking.

Despite his illness, Fraser Robinson remained optimistic, and his love for his family never waned.

Her father's incredible bravery undoubtedly helped to shape Michelle's character. She greatly admired his strength and generosity and followed in his footsteps, abstaining from expressing grievances whatever the pain they caused her, as she thought doing so was immoral and self-indulgent.[13]

More than anything in her life, including her advanced degrees from the best universities and the fact that she is married to the president of the United States, Michelle feels most proud of her family. She admires most that her parents stressed education, fostered independence of thought, brought up their children within a safe structure, were consistent in their requirements, made sure that Michelle and Craig did their daily chores, budgeted their time and money, and instead of watching television, engaged the whole family in playing board games like Monopoly every Saturday night. But she feels the most pride of all in the unselfish role model her father was as a parent, in the dream he dared to dream for his children, and his determination to keep on working, whatever the obstacles, to make sure his dream would come true.

Many people see Michelle as a perfectionist, but actually Craig is much more so than his sister. According to Michelle, he was always preparing for a disaster. It would be amusing if it weren't so tragic. For example, he practiced how he would carry his father downstairs, in case of a fire. He also staggered around the house blindfolded, so he would know what to do if he became blind. His wise mother explained that he always prepared for a disaster because his father had been struck by one, and Craig assumed it was only a matter of time until something similar happened to him, so he'd better be prepared for it. He even practiced writing with his left hand, in case something happened to the right one.[14] (Had he heard stories of his great-grandfather, Fraser Robinson Sr., whose left arm had been amputated as a child?)

Contrary to the teachings of the professor who said that MS has no silver lining, both Michelle and Craig learned lessons of great value from their father's manner of facing his illness. It taught them that if he could get up and go to work and still conduct his affairs as if all was well, they didn't have to allow the exigencies of life to restrain them either. Life tolerates no excuses and goes on without us, whatever our setbacks. So, we must soldier on, regardless of the obstacles.

One of Craig's favorite jokes about the young Michelle was that she never would find a husband whose standards approached her father's. Craig said that was the kind of man she was looking for, but she would never find one, because they didn't come like him anymore. She wanted a man who looked at the world as a half-filled glass, not one that was half empty, and men like that were hard to find. Craig was wrong. Michelle found Barack Obama, whose motto is "Yes, we can." Barack seems to love and revere the memory of Fraser as much as his children do. In his speech on middle class tax fairness, Obama said there is a place for every American in the economy of the United States, and the further we extend that window of opportunity, the more the country will gain.

"We know in this country that opportunity doesn't come easy, and we have to work for what we get," Barack added. "Here I think of my father-in-law, Fraser Robinson," Obama continued. "He raised two children with his wife Marian in 1960s Chicago," where they faced "both hidden and overt forms of racism that limited their effort to get ahead. They also faced an additional obstacle. At age 30, Fraser was diagnosed with multiple sclerosis. And yet, every day of his life . . . he went to work at the local water filtration plant while Marian stayed home with the children. And on that single salary, Fraser Robinson provided for his family, sending my wife Michelle and her brother Craig to Princeton."[15]

The Robinson family was not alone in its efforts to get ahead. Their story is repeated numerous times daily all over the country. The Robinson story is the tale of a society that values work, and of people who labor to create a better future for their families and themselves.

In a touching testimony to her love for her father, Michelle said in her Denver speech at the 2008 Democratic National Convention, "My dad was our rock. And although he was diagnosed with multiple sclerosis in his early 30s, he was our provider. He was our champion, our hero. But as he got sicker, it got harder for him to walk. It took him longer to get dressed in the morning . . . but if he was in pain, he never let on. He never stopped smiling and laughing, even while struggling to button his shirt, even while using two canes to hobble across the room to give my mom a kiss. He just woke up a little earlier and he worked a little harder.

"He and my mom poured everything they had into me and Craig. It was the greatest gift a child could receive, never doubting for a single minute that you're loved and cherished and have a place in this world. And thanks to their faith and their hard work, we both were able to go to college."[16] Robinsons' neighbor, Mrs. Credit, remembers Fraser as a man with a quick smile, even when he had greatly deteriorated with MS. She said, "He had those crutches, and it was sad to see him like that." Credit added that Fraser was a joking man and could always find something to laugh about.[17]

Fraser Robinson III died in his mid-50s in 1991, the year before Barack and Michelle Obama were married. How sad that Michelle's great hero could not have survived to see his beloved daughter become first lady of the land! Then he would have known for sure that all those bitter wintry mornings he struggled to button his shirt and hobble to work were not in vain.

NOTES

1. Jodi Kantor, "Nation's Many Faces in Extended First Family," *New York Times*, January 26, 2009.

2. David J. Garrow, "How American Ghettos Were Made; Race, Real Estate and the Black Migration to Chicago," *Washington Post*, March 15, 2009.

3. Liza Mundy, *Michelle: A Biography* (New York: Simon & Schuster, 2008), 26.

4. Lee Cary, "Obama Learned Power Politics from the Daleys," *American Thinker*, June 13, 2009.

5. Mundy, *Michelle: A Biography*, 27.

6. David Colbert, *Michelle Obama: An American Story* (Boston: Houghton Mifflin, 2009), 12.

7. Ibid.

8. Ibid.

9. Ibid.

10. Richard Wolffe, *Renegade: The Making of a President* (New York: Crown, 2009), 33.

11. Heather Boerner and Bridget Murray Law, "Heather KB, Patients Like Me. Tackling Fatigue," *Momentum*, Winter 07–08.

12. Ibid.

13. Melinda Henneberger, "The Obama Marriage: How Does It Work for Michelle Obama?" *Slate Magazine*, October 26, 2007, http://www.slate.com/id/2176683.

14. Helman, Scott. "Holding Down the Obama Family fort, 'Grandma' makes the race possible." Boston, March 30, 2008.

15. Barack Obama, "Tax Fairness for the Middle Class," remarks in Washington, D.C., September 18, 2007.

16. Michelle Obama, remarks at the Democratic National Convention, Denver, Colorado, August 25, 2008.

17. Mundy, *Michelle: A Biography*, 41.

Chapter 4

MICHELLE'S BROTHER, CRAIG

Craig Robinson was born on April 21, 1962, 21 months before the birth of Michelle. She and Craig resembled each other so closely that people often mistook them for twins. They have always been very close, and Michelle feels he was always behind her, no matter what she was doing. So, of course, during all her campaigns for Barack, Craig was with her every step of the way.

From the beginning, both Robinson children were very bright. Like Michelle, Craig learned to read at home by the age of four and skipped the second grade in school. He attended the Catholic Mount Carmel High School and graduated in 1979. He did well in both elementary and high school. Striving for the best was always the goal in the Robinson household.

Craig believes he was well brought up. Michelle and Craig were both loved and disciplined, and the family spent much of their free time together. Marian and Fraser Robinson functioned very well together as parents and taught the children how a happy home operates. Fraser came home for dinner, along with everyone else in the family, and frank, outspoken Marian shared her children's love of their home. Both children were expected to complete their chores.

"We alternated washing dishes. I had Monday, Wednesday, Friday. Michelle had Tuesday, Thursday, Saturday," Craig said.

The smoothly running, loving household may seem unusual to some of us, but according to Craig, his family was not unique.

"We were like every other family," he said. "Having loving parents is not all that unusual. People went to work then as they do now, and they counted on us to get good grades. Other mothers were at home in the neighborhood, too, so if you broke a window you were found out through the grape vine."

"Without being immodest, we were always smart, we were always driven and we were always encouraged to do the best you can do, not just what's necessary," he said.

Michelle was an impatient young girl. Craig says with only a little resentment that she used to wake him up early, "and I mean early" on Christmas morning. This was important, because they both had to be up at the same time, to be allowed to open their presents. He also says that when he was anxious, she would play the piano for him, in order to calm him down.

Both Robinson offspring were proud that their parents encouraged independent thinking and brought their children up within a safe consistent structure. Instead of watching television, the whole family played board games. When Craig challenged Michelle in Monopoly, he had to "let her win enough that she wouldn't quit."[1]

"My sister is a poor sport," he said, in one of his few uncomplimentary remarks about Michelle. "She didn't like to lose."[2] Despite her being a poor sport, however, nobody can say Michelle Robinson Obama didn't turn out well.

The Robinsons talked to Michelle and Craig about racial prejudice and taught them that they were as good as anyone else. They pointed out that life isn't always fair and you don't always get what you deserve. But you have to work hard to get what you want, and sometimes, even then, you don't get it. Craig said that seemed very unfair to him, but it prepared him for reality. The Robinsons also taught Craig and Michelle that the best way to handle prejudice is to get a good education. The two learned that lesson superbly. Having parents who constantly told their children how smart and good they were and how successful they were going to be helped them feel self-confident.

Michelle's love and admiration for her big brother is evident in the speech she presented at the Democratic National Convention in Denver in 2008. "As you might imagine," she said, "for Barack, running for president is nothing compared to that first game of basketball with my brother, Craig. I can't tell you how much it means to have Craig and my mom here tonight. Like Craig, I can feel my dad looking down on us, just as I've felt his presence in every grace-filled moment of my life.

"And at six-foot-six, I've often felt like Craig was looking down on me, too, literally. But the truth is, both when we were kids and today, Craig wasn't looking down on me; he was watching over me. And he has been there for me every step of the way since that clear day in February, 19 months ago, when, with little more than our faith in each other and a hunger for change, we joined my husband, Barack Obama, on the improbable journey that has led us to this moment.

"But each of us comes here also by way of our own improbable journey. I come here tonight as a sister, blessed with a brother who is my mentor, my protector, and my lifelong friend."

When Michelle first started dating Barack Obama, she wanted to get a second opinion on him. She thought there would be no better way than to check with basketball coach Craig, so she asked him to test Barack on the basketball court to see what kind of guy he was when he wasn't around her. Barack was not a newcomer to the sport, as he had played basketball in high school; so, Craig invited him and a few of his own friends to play pickup hoops in Chicago. Presumably, Barack was unaware that he was being tested out as a marital partner for the coach's sister, or even the cool Obama might have stressed out.

Craig was the nervous one and was very jittery about carrying out Michelle's request. He had met Barack a few times before and was rooting for him, but felt weighted down with responsibility. He worried about whether the young man would hold up in a basketball game, and didn't want to denigrate him in Michelle's eyes if he turned out to be a cad on the court. If so, Craig knew, he would have no choice but to tell her about it. But Craig always took care of his little sister, so he rolled up his sleeves "to do the obnoxious big-brother thing." Michelle was very choosy about the men she dated, and they rarely lasted very long. Craig was concerned that she never would settle down with anyone, so he particularly didn't want to rule out a man in whom she seemed interested.

Fortunately, Barack handled everything perfectly. He wasn't the best player on the court, but he wasn't the worst either. Craig found his future brother-in-law confident without being cocky, very team-oriented and unselfish. He fit in with the other players, and nobody would have known from his playing that he was the president of the *Harvard Law Review*. What Craig liked most about Barack was that when they were on the same team, Barack didn't pass Craig the ball every single time.

"He wasn't trying to suck up to my sister through me," Craig said. "I was relieved to give my sister the good news. 'Your boy is straight, and he can ball,'" he told her.[3]

Craig believes that basketball is very therapeutic for Barack. It always puts him in a good mood, and he looks forward to a game. On Election Day, he played with about 40 men in Chicago. They formed an unspoken nonaggression pact, because everyone was scared to death of giving him a big fat lip to be flashed around the world when he presented his inauguration speech. Also, the players themselves didn't want to sprain an ankle or get hurt in any way that would keep them from the inauguration. They set up four teams and played a gentle round-robin tournament.

When asked how Barack had performed on the court on Election Day, Craig quipped, "Let's just say he fared better on election night than he did in hoops earlier that day."

If asked what Barack's game says about him and how he will lead the country, Craig answers that Barack is competitive but unselfish, which he (Craig) believes is the greatest compliment you can pay a basketball player, as well as the head of a government.

There is another debt Michelle, along with the rest of the United States, owes to Craig Robinson. In 2006, when Barack Obama was considering running for president, he was aware that both Michelle and her mother were worried for his life, and also what the vigorous campaign would do to his two young daughters. So, he asked Craig as a special favor to talk with his sister and mother about the need to follow one's dreams. Craig did so and was able to convince the women that running for president was the right thing for Barack to do.

There was a time when Michelle Robinson was known as Craig Robinson's little sister, but somewhere along the line that changed.

Craig thinks it might have been after his team defeated the University of California, Davis, and he was shaking hands with a player on the opposing team. The man said, "I just want to let you know that I am voting for your brother-in-law." That may well have been when Craig realized he was now viewed as Michelle Obama's sibling, when it used to be the other way around.

When asked how he felt about being the president's brother-in-law, Craig answered, "It is mind-boggling that there is a black president. Then you layer on top of it that I am related to him? And then you layer on top of that that it's my brother-in-law? It is so overwhelming I can't hardly think about it."[4]

Despite his humility, Craig Robinson is a person to be reckoned with. He is a man who has seen how education and basketball can change a person's life, the history of a family, the history of America itself. "My motivation was our parents," Craig said.[5] "They trained us to get top grades, and we were not about to disappoint them." The Robinsons also taught Craig and Michelle not to get shaped by color, race, or the prejudice of others. Instead, they were raised to believe they are as good as anybody, and success is based upon nothing but hard work and persistence. They learned their lessons well, and basketball became the passport to success for Craig Robinson.

When he went to Mt. Carmel High School, he attended a summer basketball camp. There, one of the directors knew somebody at Princeton University and told Craig he would use his influence to get the boy admitted to the Ivy League school.

"The Ivy League? What's the Ivy League?" was Craig's response.

Craig applied to and was accepted at Princeton. Backed by his father, in the summer of 1979, carrying one suitcase and a duffel bag aboard a bus from New York City, Craig headed toward the ivy-covered walls of Princeton.

Away from his sheltering family, Craig felt completely lost. What bothered him most was that kids were pulling up in showy new cars all around him, and it seemed that all the students were carrying fans to cool their rooms. Craig didn't have a fan. He had never even thought of getting a fan. He felt absolutely overwhelmed by Princeton.

He struggled through the whole first semester, and finally called his father for advice.

"I'm in over my head here, Dad," he said.

Fraser Robinson answered, "You are not going to be number one at Princeton, but you're not going to be last either." So, Craig remained at the university, Ivy League or not.

Just as she had followed him in birth order, Michelle came to Princeton two years after her brother. Craig explained it differently. He said, "Her attitude was, 'I've always been smarter than my brother and if he can get in I can, too.'" She was right, in the latter instance, anyway.

Craig became a big man on campus twice at Princeton, when he was named Ivy player of the year. After graduating with a degree in sociology, he was drafted by the Philadelphia 76ers and spent two years playing for them overseas. He then got a master's degree in finance from the University of Chicago.

A family man like his father, Craig decided he needed to make more money to support his wife and two children adequately. So, in 1992, he went to work for a millionaire bond trader on Wall Street, Morgan Stanley Dean Witter. He was highly successful there and promoted to vice president of sales and trading. Probably because he missed his hometown and family and friends, he moved back to Chicago in 1999, where he was appointed managing director at the boutique firm of Loop Capital Markets.

Again, Craig was very successful. He said, "I have a six-bedroom house and fancy cars. I'm embarrassed to admit that I had a Porsche 944 Turbo, and a BMW station wagon. Why would you buy a $75,000 BMW station wagon? It's the dumbest car in the world." Craig Robinson was rich, but not happy. "My folks always said that if you take a job based on the pay, ultimately you're not gonna make enough money to put up with the mess." When she sensed her brother was unhappy, Michelle encouraged him to return to teaching and coaching.[6]

Craig often enjoyed helping out a few local teams, and in the back of his mind suspected he would end up coaching a seventh-grade team somewhere. The idea appealed to him more than money in the bank. "After you have a big house and snazzy car and taken all the great vacations you and your family want, you ask yourself 'now what?'" he said. "Working for money was just a job, not my passion."

One day, Bill Carmody, Craig's assistant coach at Princeton, who was the new coach at Northwestern, called and asked Craig if he wanted to be his assistant. Craig was on the trading floor. Taking a break, he hailed a taxi and rode around for a half hour to think about it.

The rest is history. At the age of 37, Craig Robinson left his high-paying job to take the low-pay job of Carmody's assistant coach. At the time, Craig was going through a divorce and had been given custody of his two small children. Like his sister, he took a pay cut equal to 90 percent of his former salary. "I have never regretted my decision," he said, "and now I can say truly I love every day of my life."

Craig remarried in June 2006. He and his new wife Kelly became very active in Barack's campaign. Since then, Craig has given many interviews telling how his sister asked him to take Obama with him to play pickup basketball, as a litmus test of his character.

"That was back when I had more cachet than Barack," Craig said.[7] "If your husband could look at the life Craig's leading right now, what do you think would be filling him with the most pride?" Jim Axelrod asked Marian Robinson in an interview for "CBS Sunday Morning" in March 2009. "He was crazy about that child before he did anything in life," Marian said. "You would not be able to stand to be in the same room with my husband right now because he thought he had the greatest kids that God ever gave anyone, and he just thought that the minute they were born."

"So he wouldn't be surprised by anything either of the kids have done?"

"No, he would not."

"Not even first lady?"

"Well, that would surprise anybody!" she laughed.

"Michelle Obama used to be Craig Robinson's little sister, because of basketball," Axelrod said. "Now you're her big brother."

"Now I'm Michelle Obama's brother and I love every minute of it," Craig said. "And I'm proud to be the coach of the Oregon State men's basketball team."

NOTES

1. Interview with Craig Robinson, *New York Times,* 2007, quoted in Rachel L. Swarns, "Family Mainstay to Move In to White House," *New York Times,* January 9, 2009, http://www.nytimes.com/2009/01/10/us/politics/10marian.html.

2. Ibid.

3. Ibid.

4. Jodi Kantor, "First Family, a Nation of Many Faces," *New York Times*, January 21, 2009.

5. Ibid.

6. "Craig Robinson, First Coach," *CBS News*, March 4, 2009, http://www.cbsnews.com/stories/2009/03/01/sunday/main4836652.shtml.

7. Ibid.

Chapter 5

THE EDUCATION OF MICHELLE OBAMA

Michelle Obama was raised by a family that had long championed education as the best path to success, and she has acknowledged the impact her education had on her life. Let us look at the educational path she followed from early childhood on and see how it led to where she is today.

As we have seen, Michelle and Craig had a head start on other children of their ages, as their mother woke them up at 4:30 every morning to teach them their alphabet and arithmetic. By the time they got to first grade, they already could read. Both children were highly motivated students from the beginning.[1] As Craig said, they always were smart, determined to do their best, and constantly encouraged to do so by their parents. The family was of one mind that the children should attend the best schools available.

Michelle began her school career at Bryn Mawr Elementary School. She developed good study habits very early in life and did so well she skipped the second grade. Skipping second grade seemed to run in the family. Mother, father, and brother, as well as Michelle, made the leap from first to third grade.

Surely it was gifts of character as well as intelligence that ensured Michelle's success at so young an age. Her hard-working parents were excellent role models. They had high expectations for their children, and Michelle did not want to let them down. Nor did she want to be disappointed in herself, and worked hard even as a little girl to make sure she received no grade lower than an A. Michelle had other interests besides studying, which she carried out as intensively. Her great-aunt was her piano teacher, and Michelle practiced the piano relentlessly, as she did everything else. Her mother said, "She would practice piano for so long you'd have to tell her to stop."[2]

Contributing to Michelle's originality, no doubt, was her mother's philosophy that, important as reading and writing are, learning to think for oneself is even more valuable. She taught her children not to swallow whole everything their teachers told them, but to judge for themselves in each instance if it was correct. This unusual mother told Michelle and Craig not even to believe everything their parents said and to be unafraid to question them about anything at all. Marian's teachings took and can be seen today in the frank and open words of the first lady, and unto the third generation, when Sasha and Malia similarly speak their minds.

Michelle went on racking up A's in regular classes until she reached the sixth grade, when the Bryn Mawr Elementary School was given a grant to open a program for gifted students. Michelle, of course, was selected for the program. There she had the opportunity to take advanced courses, such as French and biology, at the local community college, Kennedy-King. The classes were truly extraordinary for middle school students, who were perhaps 12 or 13 years of age. For example, in a science laboratory, Michelle and her fellow students dissected rats to learn how muscles function. In terms of theory, they studied such subjects as photosynthesis, the cellular interaction with light that is fundamental to all plant life. A far cry from the subjects followed in general education classes! When Michelle graduated from middle school with honors in 1977, she was appointed salutatorian (best scholar) of her class.

Michelle and her parents then discussed ad infinitum what high school she should attend. Should she go to a neighborhood high school? Convenient as that would be, the answer was no, as schools largely attended by African American students were often lacking in good books, supplies, resources, and even dedicated and well-trained teachers. Fortunately, another option opened up for Michelle at the decisive moment: the chance to attend a new kind of school, a magnet high school, available to qualified students of all races. These schools featured clubs and extra-curricular activities not generally found in high schools attended by minority students and gave graduates the chance to be admitted to top universities.

In 1977, Michelle Robinson was enrolled in the ninth grade at Whitney M. Young Magnet High School. The student body was a melting pot of elite youths of many classes and races from all sections of Chicago. Although there was a high school only a block from the Robinson home, Michelle's parents encouraged her to take the long bus rides to and from the magnet school.

It was courageous of the 13-year-old girl to take long trips into an unknown industrial territory twice a day. But Michelle was so happy about the school that she didn't mind the long trek, and probably used the time to good avail doing homework and studying. She found the school warm and accepting, and blossomed there both academically and socially. Michelle took and passed advanced courses and made the honor roll all four years she was at Whitney Young. She was accepted into the National Honor Society, served as treasurer of the student council, and was an active member of the fund-raising publicity committee. All in all, she was a most desirable contender for many colleges. But Michelle would not have been satisfied with just any college. She wanted to reach the top, to attend an Ivy League college. Unfortunately, she failed to attract the attention of her school's college counselors, who were able to help the top students gain admission into prestigious universities.

Although Michelle had worked hard and got excellent grades, she did not graduate at the top of her class and had earned a class ranking of only 32. She had attained that position among the graduates only because she had worked tremendously hard at her studies. For one thing, she had difficulty scoring well on tests. This was in contrast to her brother Craig, who seemed to sail through his classes without touching a book. His mother said, "She had a brother who could pass a test just by carrying a book under his arm." Craig's admission into Princeton made Michelle determined to get in, too. She said she knew him and his study habits, and if he could get into Princeton, she could, too. As she said, "Every time somebody told me, 'No, you can't do that,' I pushed past their doubts and I took my seat at the table."[3] Thus, Michelle Robinson took her seat at the table of Princeton University.

Michelle believes, according to what a campaign spokeswoman told *Newsweek,* that she was given a boost in admission to Princeton not by affirmative action but because she was the sister of Craig Robinson, a "big man on campus."[4] If true, this made her a legacy admission, along with the many white students for whom Princeton was a family tradition. But Michelle determined to prove that no matter what help she had received, she richly deserved to be in the class.

Located in a leafy green suburb, the great university with its gothic granite buildings on manicured green lawns must have caused culture shock in the teenager from the packed South Side of Chicago, living away from her parents for the first time. At that time, the Princeton population included only 16 percent of minority students, and for the first time in her young life Michelle had to confront the problems inherent in being one of a minority group, 1 of 94 black students in a class of 1,141 freshmen.

Of all the Ivy League colleges, Princeton in the 1980s was considered the most preppy by no less an authority than the *Official Preppy Handbook* (1980). By the time Michelle was admitted, obvious discrimination against minorities had gone underground. Segregation was prohibited by law even in the South. Nevertheless, enough underlying racial prejudice remained at the university to make Michelle feel like an outsider. She e-mailed the *Boston Globe,* "Sometimes that's the thing you sense, that there's something that's there, but it's unspoken." At Princeton, she came to terms with being a black achiever in a white world.[5]

Her social life was made a bit easier because she was the sister of Craig, the "big man on campus." She got to know a lot of people because of him. But Craig was afraid that his presence might have put a damper on her dating life, as the fellows were aware that he was keeping a big brotherly eye on his little sister.[6]

Michelle Obama's senior thesis at Princeton University, "Princeton-Educated Blacks and the Black Community," is a testimony to a young woman's belief that a black Princeton student was permitted only on the periphery of college life. "My experiences at Princeton have made me far more aware of my 'blackness' than ever before," she wrote in her introduction. She added that she sometimes felt "like a visitor on campus; as if I really don't belong. Regardless of the circumstances under which I interact with whites at Princeton, it often seems as if, to them, I will always be black first and a student second."

A sociology major, Michelle explored her feelings about being a member of a minority group at college in her thesis. In the introduction, Michelle wondered what impact going to a mostly white college had upon the self-images of black students, whether they felt more comfortable with blacks or whites before and after they attended Princeton. To research the question, she sent out hundreds of questionnaires to African American Princeton graduates, asking them how they felt about white people before and after attending the university. She also asked her subjects how their college experiences had made them feel about themselves and other blacks.

The 96-page dissertation in 1985 became the object of much speculation after it was temporarily withdrawn from Princeton's library until after the presidential election.[7] People, of course, wondered why it was withdrawn and what in it is so radical that no one is allowed to see it.

The treatise is a glimpse into the mind and heart of the young Michelle Obama, who as an adult passionately supported Barack Obama's presidential ambitions and who made the controversial remark, "For the first time in my adult lifetime, I am really proud of my country." The thesis is a treasure chest bursting with Michelle Robinson's feelings as a young woman. It is possible that, were the thesis written today, the philosophy of the mature first lady might be different.

"In defining the concept of identification or the ability to identify with the black community," Michelle wrote, "I based my definition on the premise that there is a distinctive black culture very different from white culture." The young woman perceived racially insensitive behavior in a university comprised mostly of Caucasian educators and students: "Predominately white universities like Princeton," she wrote, "are socially and academically designed to cater to the needs of the white students comprising the bulk of their enrollments."

She noted that the university engaged only five black tenured pro-fessors and that the "Afro-American studies program was one of the smallest and most understaffed departments in the university." In ad-dition, she said that Princeton had only one recognized group for the intellectual development of black and third world students, and that the university was "infamous for being racially the most conservative of the Ivy League universities."

In a section concerning her views on the political relationship be-tween blacks and whites, Michelle quoted sociologists James Conyers and Walter Wallace on the "integration of black official(s) into various aspects of politics." She discussed "problems which face these black of-ficials who must persuade the white community that they are above is-sues of race and that they are representing all people and not just black people." The same task faces the president and Mrs. Obama today. Ac-cording to Valerie Jarrett, special adviser to the president and longtime friend of both Obamas, Michelle "will reach out to the full spectrum of American people." Jarrett continued, "That's what she's done through-out her whole life—embrace all ethnicities. I believe there will be a special connection with the African American community, because she's the first African American first lady. Michelle's heart has plenty of room for everybody."[8]

In order to research her thesis, Michelle sent a questionnaire to 400 African American graduates of Princeton. She requested them to define the time and level of comfort they had experienced with both races before becoming students at the school, as well as during and after their years there. She included questions dealing with careers, religious beliefs, living arrangements, role models, economic status, and feelings toward blacks of lower classes. The subjects also were asked whether they would consider themselves as having a separationist or an assimilationist point of view. Fewer than 90 alumni, or 22 percent, of those sent Michelle's questionnaire answered. Surprisingly, their conclusions were different from those she had anticipated. She had hoped that despite their high degree of identification with whites, the alumni "would still maintain a certain level of identification with the black community. However," she concluded, "these findings do not support this possibility."

Some people feel that Michelle's thesis is a disguised argument for racial separatism. Christopher Hitchens in an article for *Slate*, an online magazine, believes this to be true because Michelle drew upon the arguments of Stokely Carmichael (Kwame Ture), the Black Nationalist, in her thesis. According to Liza Mundy, however, Hitchens is incorrect in his assumption. She believes that Michelle quoted Carmichael only to use his definition of separationism in order to explore his concept of assimilationism.[9]

Despite her feelings of being a "visitor on campus," as her thesis describes, Michelle graduated from Princeton with honors in 1985. According to several professors and friends, Michelle's Princeton years were a point around which her identity was formed. As her advisor at Harvard Law School, Professor Charles J. Ogletree, recalled, "Princeton was a real crossroads of identity for Michelle" as she wondered if her education at an elite university would change the identity she had inherited from her African American parents.[10]

In simpler terms, Michelle was afraid that Princeton would change her values from her need to serve the black community to striving for the same goals as her white classmates, of entering a distinguished graduate school or accepting a high-paying position in a prestigious corporation.

"By the time she got to Harvard," Dr. Ogletree surmised, "she had answered the question. She could be both brilliant and black."

Michelle had worked hard at Princeton and graduated with honors. She entered Harvard Law School in 1985. This time around, there was no doubt in her mind that she had earned her place in the illustrious school.

Her new sense of self-confidence was evident to everyone around her. A Harvard classmate spoke of Michelle as having an incredible presence. "She's very, very smart, very charismatic, very well spoken."[11] The ability to state an argument clearly and succinctly is a necessary skill for becoming a successful attorney. Michelle, who was trained to present her case around the dinner table while growing up in Chicago, had already demonstrated as a child that she had this aptitude.

Michelle was a student in Professor David B. Wilkins's legal profession class, in which he asked the class how they would behave in difficult legal and ethical situations. While many pupils were shy about exposing themselves in this way, Wilkins said that Michelle "always stated her position clearly and decisively."[12] Anyone who knows her could have predicted that Michelle Robinson, who was so frank and open in all aspects of her life, would behave similarly in Professor Wilkins's class.

Despite her busy schedule, Michelle devoted time to address the problem she discussed in her thesis by providing legal help to poor people in the Boston and Cambridge areas. The service was essentially a student-run law firm, where the members committed themselves to work at least 20 hours a week. Michelle fought for people who were being unfairly evicted and for women who needed assistance in getting a divorce or winning custody of their children. Robert Torbert, a classmate who worked with Michelle at the Harvard Legal Aid Bureau, said, "She was very mature, very bright. She handled some of the more complex landlord-and-tenant issues. I just remember her being very serious about the work she did, and she really cared about the people she worked with."[13] Michelle also worked with the law school to attract more African American students and participated in demonstrations calling for more minority professors and students.

Michelle also joined African American organizations at Harvard Law School, as she had at Princeton. One group to which she belonged was the Black Law Students Association. This group arranged meetings with black Harvard Law School alumni, who described the shape their careers had taken after they graduated. In this way, the students learned of possible careers they could follow, whether lawyers in private practice, government employees, or public service. First lady of the United States was not one of the possibilities mentioned.

Michelle, like the other members of her class, was deeply preoccupied with thoughts of what she would do after graduation. As previously stated, she was concerned that she would lose the values by which she had been raised. For a while, it seemed that had happened, as she joined Sidley & Austin, a large corporate law firm. The high starting salary would help pay off her school debts, and in addition, take her back to Chicago, her beloved hometown, where she would rejoin the family that she missed so much.

How did Michelle feel about returning to Chicago as an accomplished woman with degrees from two of the top universities in the country? According to Valerie Jarrett, Michelle's mentor and friend who became one of Barack Obama's advisers, Michelle "takes a great deal of pride in saying, 'I've done better than maybe people thought I would have done.'"[14]

NOTES

1. Rosalind Rossi, "The Woman Behind Obama," *Chicago Sun-Times*, January 20, 2007.

2. Karen Springen, "First Lady in Waiting," *Chicago* magazine, October 2004.

3. Jay Newton-Small, "Michelle Obama Finds Her Voice Too," *Time*, January 24, 2008.

4. Richard Wolffe, "Barack's Rock," Newsweek, February 5, 2008.

5. Sally Jacobs, "Learning to be Michelle Obama," Boston Globe, June 15, 2008.

6. Liza Mundy, *Michelle: A Biography* (New York: Simon & Schuster, 2008), 72.

7. André Leon Talley, "Leading Lady," Vogue.com, March 2009.

8. Jonah Goldberg, National Review Online, February 19, 2008.

9. Mundy, *Michelle: A Biography*, 17.

10. Sally Jacobs, "Learning to be Michelle Obama," *Boston Globe*, June 15, 2008, http://www.boston.com/news/nation/articles/2008/06/15/learning_to_be_michelle_obama/.

11. David Bergen Brophy, *Michelle Obama: Meet the First Lady* (New York: HarperCollins, 2009), 34–36.

12. Ibid.

13. Ibid.

14. Claire Shipman, Susan Ricci, and Emily Yacus, "Michelle's Passions: Wife, Mother, Intellectual, American Woman," *ABC News*, July 7, 2008, quoted in Elizabeth Lightfoot, *Michelle Obama, First Lady of Hope* (Guilford, CT: Lyons Press, 2009), 179.

Chapter 6

MICHELLE, THE CORPORATE LAWYER

Shortly after her graduation from Harvard Law School, Michelle Robinson began working full-time at Sidley & Austin, a large corporate law firm. The company handles the legal work of various types of clients and oversees many different aspects of their activities.

Michelle first became acquainted with Sidley & Austin while still a student at Harvard Law School, when she was hired by the firm as a summer intern. She enjoyed her work and did so well that she was offered a full-time position there, on graduation from Harvard Law School. She accepted the job at a beginning salary of $65,000.

When Michelle complained that the work she had been assigned to in general litigation was boring, she was placed in the marketing division, a unit of the corporation that now would be called intellectual property or entertainment law. The division represents clients who sell goods to the public, such as advertising agencies and beer and car manufacturers, and assures that clients are treated fairly and profitably by the companies that employ them. At the time, one of the division's clients was Don King, the colorful boxing promoter; another was Coors Brewing Company, which produces the favorite beer of the late, great Paul Newman. A third fun client was Barney, the purple dinosaur. Michelle's job was to produce the trademark and distribution of Barney's plush toys and other spin-offs and to negotiate with TV stations that wished to run the show. Her bosses considered Michelle's position in the Marketing Division one of the most creative of all the jobs in the firm. Nevertheless, despite working with the fun accounts, Michelle wanted to serve the community, and she felt that the work at Sidley & Austin was not up to her standards.

Her boss, Quincy White, was puzzled about Michelle. He saw that as a very ambitious woman, she was perpetually dissatisfied and wanted work that pushed her harder and was more of a challenge. White said, "I couldn't give her something that would meet her sense of ambition to change the world."[1] By this remark, he meant that Michelle wanted to change the world, but he didn't feel he could help her to do it.

Whether it was because of the racial differences or simply because she thought work and social life don't mix, Michelle said little to her colleagues about her personal life.[2] Although it was tremendously important to her and changed her life forever, Michelle never even mentioned to them that her father had died. His death was one of the most profound misfortunes she ever experienced, and it made her aware of how short life can be. She reflected, as her father would have done, "If what you are doing doesn't bring you joy every single day, what's the point?"

Michelle's first impressions of Barack Obama were not very enthusiastic. He had gotten rave reviews from some of the Sidley & Austin lawyers, and others were impressed with his fine record as a first year Harvard Law School student. He had just finished his first year at the school. Sidley & Austin did not ordinarily hire first year students as summer associates, which in itself was noteworthy. To add to all the hoopla, the secretaries raved about how handsome he was. Michelle thought he sounded too good to be true. She had met a lot of applicants with Barack's reputation and suspected he was the kind of man who could "talk straight and impress people." She was very suspicious that his glowing attributes were all on the surface and wasn't at all sure his reputation would hold up. When she heard that he had been raised in Hawaii, she presumed he would be "nerdy, strange, and off-putting," and decided that she disliked him.[3]

Nevertheless, like it or not, she had been appointed his mentor and had a job to do. She showed Barack his office and some of the procedures he would be following, and took him to lunch. He wore a sports jacket and had a cigarette hanging from his mouth. Michelle thought, "Uh oh, here's this good-looking, smooth-talking guy. I've been down this road before."[4]

Barack had a completely different reaction to their meeting. He was absolutely taken with Michelle. He liked her bright and easy laugh, and the glimmer that danced around her round dark eyes whenever he looked into them. He was able to see beneath her efficient self and detect a fragility that no one else had picked up, as if she could disintegrate if things got too rough.[5] He was very moved by what he saw and wanted to get to know that hidden part of her nature.

Michelle and Barack spent a lot of time together. Since she was his mentor, they met every day at the office or at the frequent outings held by the firm to encourage good relations among employees. They even attended a few parties together. Michelle, still professing that she was not interested in Barack as a boyfriend, arranged several dates with her friends for him. But Barack was not interested in them. He is a man who knows what he wants, and in this case, it was Michelle. He kept plying her to go out with him. She always refused, saying it was not appropriate for a mentor and mentee to date. But, all the time, she confessed later, underneath her veneer she had her eye on him. She told Katie Couric in an interview that she had liked Barack immediately because he didn't take himself too seriously. She liked that he was bright, had an interesting background different from hers, and also that he laughed a lot. She liked to talk with him and considered him a friend.

But Barack, who is nothing if not persistent, eventually wore her down, and she found it increasingly difficult to keep saying no to him. It was not his way to woo her with flowers and candy. Instead, having looked deeply into her soul, this unusual man took this unusual woman to the basement of the church where he had done some of his community service before attending Harvard Law School. Was she turned off by his choice of location for their first real date, as many young women would have been? Absolutely not! In fact, she was thrilled to watch Barack speak to the audience of mostly single African American mothers, and before her eyes turn from a law student wearing a suit and tie to an empathetic and warm-hearted person who touched the hearts of the struggling people he was addressing. This was when she first realized that Barack Obama was a very special man, a man who shared her father's values and sense of social justice. Handsome and smart as he was, it was Barack Obama's passion for helping poor African Americans that swept Michelle Robinson off her feet. It said to her that Barack shared her desire to change humanity and that together they could move mountains.

After their first date, Michelle forgot about office policy, and she and Barack spent much of their free time together. She took delight in showing him the neighborhood where she had played, attended school and church, and grew up in, and he took her to places he had frequented as a community organizer. And they talked, talked, and talked about their pasts and hoped-for futures. Their first kiss was another story. They were sitting on a curb in front of Baskin-Robbins eating chocolate ice cream cones. Barack leaned over and kissed Michelle on the lips. "It tasted like chocolate," he said.

Barack and the Robinsons met and liked each other very much. They immediately took in the rootless young man as one of their own, even to giving him a family birthday party. Marian remembered him as a quiet fellow who didn't talk about himself, who neglected to mention that he was running for president of the *Harvard Law Review*. The family had no inkling of how intelligent he is. To the boy who grew up without a father, Michelle's family seemed ideal, close knit, and supportive, with a kind, loving father who never missed a day of work or a basketball game of his son, despite Fraser's crippling illness. Barack poignantly wrote, "For someone like me, who had barely known his father, who had spent much of his life traveling from place to place, his bloodlines scattered to the four winds, the home that Fraser and Marian Robinson built for themselves and their children stirred a longing for stability and a sense of place that I had not realized was there."[6]

Although no official announcement of an engagement had been made, there was no doubt in Michelle's and Barack's minds that they were in a committed relationship, in which they dated each other exclusively. But the strength of the connection between the two was put to the test when Barack left Chicago in the fall to complete his final two years at Harvard Law School. The two continued the relationship by frequent phone calls, exchanging letters, and occasionally meeting for a weekend either in Chicago or Cambridge.

In the meantime, Michelle continued working at Sidley & Austin, at a job she found less and less gratifying. She told a *Newsweek* reporter that people at the firm, although happy to have their jobs, didn't bound out of bed in the morning eager to get to work. Michelle couldn't see going through life without bounding out of bed in the morning eager to get on with the day. She needed to have a career built on passion and not just money. And she had to know that she was doing good for others, as well as herself. None of this was happening at Sidley & Austin.

The couple conducted a long-distance romance. That didn't make Michelle too happy, so she pressured Barack to get married. She told a reporter from the *New Yorker* that she and Barack had a running debate throughout that part of their relationship about the merits of marriage. She announced to her reluctant fiancé, "Look, buddy, I'm not one of those who will just hang out forever." He answered, "Marriage, it doesn't mean anything, it's really how you feel." Michelle answered, "Yeah, right."[7]

This all changed in 1991. One night while dining at Gordon's, an elegant Chicago restaurant, they began arguing about marriage again. At the end of the meal, however, a plate with an engagement ring arrived—and Michelle was too shocked and embarrassed to say a word. "That kind of shuts you up, doesn't it?" Barack asked.[8]

In case any doubts remain, the incident makes clear that Barack has a terrific sense of humor and is unintimidated by Michelle, beautiful, intelligent, and strong as she is.

Then, a great sorrow came into Michelle's life. In 1991, her beloved father, a man only in his mid-50s, suddenly passed away after kidney surgery. Michelle and her family were heartbroken, and Barack flew into Chicago to give his emotional support to his fiancée, who rested her head on his shoulder during the funeral. While watching the burial, Barack silently promised Fraser Robinson that he would take care of his daughter.[9]

The death of a father is a landmark event in a person's life that often causes profound changes in the bereaved child. So it was with Michelle Robinson, who searched her soul at its deepest levels after her father died. She wondered if she had chosen her career wisely. If she were to die in four months, she mused, would she feel she had spent her life in a satisfactory manner? Was she benefiting the community that had made her, in a manner that would please her father? The answer to the questions she asked herself was an unequivocal "No!"

Shortly after her self-questioning, Michelle made a formidable change in her life. Accepting a significant decrease in salary, she left Sidley & Austin and the practice of corporate law to take a position on Chicago Mayor Richard Daley's staff. On the death of a beloved person, a bereaved individual often comforts himself or herself by identifying with the deceased. Fraser Robinson had experienced great satisfaction by working as a Democratic Party precinct captain. Michelle Robinson followed in her father's footsteps and took a job with the Democratic Party. She was named Economic Development Coordinator of Chicago's Department of Planning and Development. As the coordinator between the city administration and people attempting to build their businesses, she helped Chicago's small business men and women to prosper. Michelle said in an interview with the *New York Times* that after her father died she had looked out at the neighborhood and had an epiphany that she had to bring her skills to bear in the place that had made her.[10] It was a move into public service that proved central to her career and her life.

In October 1992, a radiant Michelle Robinson married Barack Obama in the Trinity United Church of Christ. The ceremony was performed by the Reverend Jeremiah Wright. Santita Jackson, daughter of the Reverend Jesse Jackson and Michelle's long-time friend, sang at the wedding. The newlyweds went on a honeymoon to California, and then resided for a few months with Michelle's mother in the Robinson family home. They then took an apartment of their own, a walk-up condominium in Chicago's politically progressive Hyde Park.

While they lived in Hyde Park, Michelle again changed jobs. Barack was one of the founders of Public Allies, an organization that trained young people for public service. When he left, he recommended Michelle to serve as executive director. She fell into the job as naturally as if it had been waiting for her and she for it.

No aspect of the job was beneath her. If stamps needed licking, Michelle was there. She thought nothing of door-to-door canvassing in unsafe housing projects to recruit trainees. When money was needed to fund the program, Michelle contacted wealthy donors she had met

Michelle Robinson Obama and Barack Obama at their wedding reception, October 18, 1992, in Chicago. (AP Photo/Obama for America.)

while working at Sidley & Austin and the Mayor's office to ask for donations.

Despite the huge reduction in salary, Michelle at last found herself "happy to leap out of bed in the morning." She said her work with Public Allies was the best thing she had done in her professional career.[11]

"It was the first thing that was mine," she said, "and I was responsible for every aspect of it. My passions and talents converged."

In 1996, Barack ran for and was elected Illinois state senator from Chicago's 13th district. The legislature is located in Springfield, the state capital, 200 miles from their home. His election meant that Barack had to be away from his wife for long stretches of time. This was very upsetting to both of them, and Barack, whose slogan was "Yes, we can," wrote that they overcame the pain of the rupture by talking and laughing over the phone, sharing the humor and frustrations of their time apart. Then he would be able to fall asleep, content in the knowledge of their love. Despite the distress caused by their separation, Michelle supported Barack's run for senator, as she felt it was something he needed to do.[12]

Also, around this time, the couple decided they wanted to have a child. Realizing that she could not keep up the incredible amount of hours she put into her work at Public Allies and be the kind of mother she demanded of herself, Michelle found a replacement for her position and began looking for part-time work near her home.

The University of Chicago was nearby. Strangely enough, Michelle had never been on the campus. She said, "As a black kid on the South Side, the University of Chicago was a foreign entity to me."[13] She took her first steps on university grounds when she applied for and was hired for a job as Associate Dean of Student Services. Her goal was to involve the university students in neighborhood problems and to eliminate sexism on campus. She served on the sexual harassment policy committee, where a colleague said Michelle was great at the job, as she had "a real directness and sense of humor—not bawdy, just a down-to-earth 'Let's get this done.'"[14]

July 4, 1998, was a high point in the life of Michelle and Barack Obama: their daughter and first child Malia Ann Obama was born. Later, in The Audacity of Hope (2006), the loving father wrote, "So calm and so beautiful, with big, hypnotic eyes that seemed to read the world the moment they opened."[15] Happy as Michelle was about Malia's arrival, she was still putting in many hours at her so-called part-time job. Barack, the state senator, was working very hard and still had to be away from home a great deal. He spent much of what little time he had free holed up in his office in their railroad apartment. This left Michelle feeling very lonely and resentful. They fought constantly about the situation, and the pressure they were under led to the shakiest moments in the Obama marriage.

When Natasha (Sasha) was born in 2001, things got even worse in the Obama household. Barack wrote that his wife's anger toward him was barely contained. She accused him of thinking only of himself and raged that she had never thought she would have to raise her children as a single mother.

Barack, an only child, did not realize the seriousness of his wife's accusations, and in The Audacity of Hope, he poignantly wrote, "All I asked for . . . was a little tenderness. Instead, I found myself subjected to endless negotiations about every detail of managing the house, long lists of things that I needed to do or had forgotten to do, and a generally sour attitude." It was only later that he understood the part Michelle had played in keeping the family together. Then he was able to credit her strength and willingness to manage their tensions and sacrifices that led them though the difficult times, and, indeed, preserved their marriage. She did not realize at the time that the strain this gifted man was putting through in his work as senator of the United States was a gift to their country.

It was Michelle's change of heart that solved the problem. She says, on looking back, she realized that she simply had to make the best of things if she desired to keep the family together. She knew that Barack, given his great ambitions, was unable to change, and she had no choice but to live with the situation if she were to hold the family together. She said, "I cannot be crazy, because then I'm a crazy mother and I'm an angry wife."

She secured her job at the University Medical Center in an unusual way. While on maternity leave with her second child, she said to herself, "I'll do this as a courtesy, demand a whole bunch of stuff he's not going to give me, [the university president] will say no, and we'll be done." To make the point, she went to the interview with two-month-old Sasha in her arms. "I had on a breast feeding top. I strolled in: 'Hi! This is me! New baby!' . . . And I said, 'I can't be in your office all afternoon in meetings. Also, I can't be your diversity— a nice person who could 'represent.'"[16] To her astonishment, the university said yes to everything. Michelle Obama was on her way.

NOTES

1. David Bergen Brophy, *Michelle Obama: Meet the First Lady* (New York: HarperCollins, 2009), 42.

2. Liza Mundy, *Michelle, A Biography* (New York: Simon & Schuster, 2008).

3. Ibid., 94.

4. Brophy, *Michelle Obama: Meet the First Lady*, 43–44.

5. Barack Obama, *The Audacity of Hope* (New York: Random House, 2006).

6. Ibid., 329.

7. Lauren Collins, "The Other Obama," *New Yorker*, March 10, 2008.

8. Liza Mundy, "When Michelle Met Barack," *Washington Post*, October 5, 2008, http://www.washingtonpost.com/wp-dyn/content/article/2008/09/26/AR2008092602856.html?sid=ST2008100302144.

9. Obama, *The Audacity of Hope*.

10. Michael Powell and Jodi Kantor, "After Attacks, Michelle Obama Looks for a New Introduction," *New York Times*, June 18, 2008.

11. "In October, 1992 . . . " *Times of India*, Barack Obama's marriage was on brink of collapse: Book, June 7, 2009.

12. Geraldine Brooks, "Michelle Obama: Camelot 2.0?," *More*, October 2008.

13. Obama, *The Audacity of Hope*, 339.

14. Brophy, *Michelle Obama: Meet the First Lady*, 65.

15. Obama, *The Audacity of Hope*.

16. Ibid., 339.

Chapter 7

THE CHARACTER OF MICHELLE OBAMA

What is Michelle Obama really like? Is she really all she seems to be? Who was it who said, "When something seems too good to be true, it usually is"? Let's take a look at Michelle's character and judge for ourselves if the anonymous philosopher is correct about Michelle Obama.

Crowds press in to get closer to her. She seems to like them back. Michelle Obama is probably the most popular first lady the United States has ever had. In contrast to the also adored Jacqueline Kennedy, who prided herself on remaining mysterious and unapproachable, Michelle is as open and frank with strangers as she is with her peers. Author Maya Angelou says Michelle is the real thing. Many people are different up close than they are with their loved ones. Not Michelle. She looks people straight in the eye when she talks to them. She even is known to wink when she smiles. She frequently hugs older women and is more likely to speak to children than adults.

"Michelle is a very down-to-earth person, who is very interested in people," according to Harriet Cole. "She is also very smart, and does whatever she sets out to do."[1]

It happened when Michelle came to the RFK Stadium to help assemble care packages for the troops in Iraq, early in her husband's presidency.

A boy called out to her over and over again, to no avail. "Miss Michelle, Miss Michelle!" But the first lady couldn't hear his tiny voice over the noises inside the stadium. Finally, someone told Sharon Henderson, the boy's mother, to yell louder. Henderson roared out Mrs. Obama's name.

Michelle Obama suddenly stopped assembling packages and looked up. She gave the boy a wide smile and waved cheerfully at mother and child.

"It meant the world to me that she would look up," Mrs. Henderson said. "She is a very warm person."[2]

Then Michelle asked a little girl what her name was.

The child replied "Maya."

Ever the educator, Michelle responded, "Do you know there is a famous poet with your name?" If Maya didn't know it before, she'll never forget it now.

Michelle then turned to a boy in a brown corduroy jacket and told him to work hard in school. Yes, he can!

Six-year-old Kennedy Walls was next to approach the first lady, and bravely asked her if Malia and Sasha could come to a ball in Arlington, Virginia. Michelle thanked the child kindly, but said her daughters are very busy.[3]

When Mrs. Obama visited Anacostia High School, where a violent melee in November had sent a number of young people to the hospital with stab wounds, she hugged the students and sat in a semicircle with 10 girls and 3 boys.

When a girl asked, "How did you get where you are now?" the first lady said, "There's no magic to being here. My parents were working class people." She said that she went to public schools just as they did, as her parents could not afford to pay for private schools, and it was mainly the support she received from them that helped her get where she is. Michelle added, "Our job is simple. Just be open, be honest, be real, be clear—and have fun."[4]

Mrs. Obama told the youngsters that even though she had lived near the University of Chicago as a child, she had never taken a "walk on campus. I didn't think they wanted to have anything to do with me, so we never connected—me and many kids like me in our community, and that big old institution." She stressed that she does not want young people today to feel similarly disconnected from the White House.

After the school visit, dozens of students were invited to have dinner at the White House with Obama and women who worked for the administration. The first lady again reminded the students that the White House is not far away. "We're close," she said. "This isn't a distant relationship. They can imagine the people who live here and what goes on here, and that there's a close connection between their lives and ours."[5]

The students then asked many questions about the Obama lifestyle and family, including daughters Malia and Sasha. When asked why the Obama girls had not come with their mother that day, Michelle replied that they were in school. She explained that, even though the girls live in the White House, they "have to get up, set their alarms, get their own breakfasts, make up their beds, and put on their clothes, and get to school on time," just like everyone else.

When asked what having the Secret Service around is like: "They bring a lot of commotion, but they're all good, good folks."

By far, the most provocative question of the day came from a young lady interested in knowing whether or not Mrs. Obama does her own makeup every day.

"Hmm," came the reply.

The student repeated her question.

"I didn't today because it was special. But most of the time I do."

"You pick your own clothes out?"

"I do," said Mrs. Obama with a smile.[6]

On their first day in the White House, the president and Mrs. Obama greeted visitors. Emotions ran high for some, including Michelle, on the Obamas' first day in their new home. A woman came up to her and said that she and her family were beautiful. Mrs. Obama asked the woman to please stop or she would begin to cry and smear her makeup. According to Jackie Norris, Michelle's chief of staff at the time, her aim as first lady is to support the values and the agenda of the president. But she does it in her own way as no other first lady before her has ever done. And the people of the United States respond enthusiastically.[7]

Even early in her husband's administration, Michelle Obama's rating was much more positive than those of her predecessors. Americans polled held overwhelmingly approving views of first lady Michelle Obama, a CBS News/New York Times poll found, with 49 percent viewing her favorably.[8] In contrast, Laura Bush's likeability rating at the beginning of her husband's term of office was 30 percent, while such ratings for Hillary Clinton were 44 percent, Barbara Bush 34 percent, and Nancy Reagan 28 percent. Michelle's ratings keep going up. At a more recent poll, her ratings were at an incredible 72 percent.

A Princeton undergraduate and Harvard Law School graduate like Barack Obama, Michelle is the first first-family-member with a degree in African American studies. Her background already has a tremendous influence on children. When Michelle was visiting a charter school, one little girl said to her, "When I grow up, I want to be first lady."

The mischievous Michelle responded, "It doesn't pay much."[9] Her mission statement in the campaign reads, "I want to help other families . . . not just to survive, but to thrive." Coming from the impoverished South Side of Chicago, she understands firsthand how life is lived in the under classes of the United States.

Michelle Obama's compassion is not restricted to African Americans, but extends to Americans of all colors and backgrounds. Early in her husband's administration, Michelle spent some time working at Miriam's Kitchen, a soup kitchen near the White House. The people she was helping were pleasantly surprised to discover who was serving them food, but none more so than Bill Richardson, a 46-year-old homeless man. Richardson was so starstruck upon seeing Mrs. Obama that he could scarcely manage to thank her.

"I was expecting some lunch, but this is the president's wife; this is her right here!" he exclaimed later. He planned to get to a phone as soon as possible to regale his mother with his story.[10]

Even nicer was Michelle's humility about her kindly action. Tony Bennett, who sang three songs at a Democratic fund-raiser, said, "I'd like to say something about our wonderful first lady." He told the audience that Michelle Obama had fed the homeless and pleaded that it not be made public. "Please, please, don't put this in the paper," she begged.[11] Apparently, the news-hungry media refused to listen to Michelle and gave out the story anyway.

Michelle Obama asked Americans to follow in her footsteps and donate a day of service to honor the birthday of Martin Luther King. She quoted him that "Everybody can be great . . . because anybody can serve. You don't have to have a college degree to serve. You don't have to make your subject and verb agree to serve. You only need a heart full of grace and a soul generated by love."[12] No doubt Americans will see a great more of these qualities before Barack and Michelle Obama leave the White House.

Despite all her sophistication and brilliance, Michelle at times has a delightful, almost childlike quality about her that usually is kept hidden from observers. For instance, she is excited when a movie star wants to see Barack, and finds it "kind of neat. . . . It's like, you're kidding, right? They are nervous, too! But you are Queen Latifah." Or when Barbara Walters came up to Michelle and said, "I just want to introduce myself to you." Michelle wanted to say, "I know who you are."[13]

A moving example of this little-known side of Michelle's personality is described in her husband's book, *The Audacity of Hope*. "I remember the first time I took Michelle to Kenya," Obama writes, "shortly before we were married." As an African American, Michelle was bursting with excitement about the idea of visiting the continent of her ancestors, and "we had a wonderful time, visiting my grandmother up-county, wandering through the streets of Nairobi, camping in the Serengeti, fishing off the island of Lamu." Unfortunately, Michelle's joy was short-lived, as she discovered "the terrible sense on the part of most Kenyans that their fates were not their own." They found it difficult to find work without bribing someone, activists were jailed for speaking their minds, and Michelle found the close ties within Barack's family suffocating, as even distant relatives constantly asked for favors. On their return flight to Chicago, Michelle told Barack that she really looked forward to getting home. "I never realized how American I was," she said, referring to how free she was and how much she appreciated her freedom.[14] Mary Todd Lincoln once said, "Men have the advantage of us women." True as Mrs. Lincoln's philosophy may be for the majority of women, both today and then, one doubts whether it can be applied to Michelle Obama.

According to Kamyra Harding, a partner at a resource development firm in Manhattan, women mold and polish their guy. "Michelle just did what we all do," Harding said. "You find this guy and you mold him, he's got the raw material, but he had to be polished before anyone would pay attention to him. You want the house, check, the little girls, check, check."[15] Harding may be right, but to mold and polish the president of the United States is a pretty impressive piece of work.

Michelle may still be "polishing up her guy." It seems she is the leader of the dog pack. On the family's first walk with their new dog, Bo, Michelle handled most of the leash duties, although Malia also took a turn. President Obama said family members will take turns walking Bo.[16] Whichever family member walks the dog, Michelle is as gracious as she is generous. According to Katie McCormick Lelyveld, Mrs. Obama's spokeswoman, Michelle brought a very thoughtful gift to Laura Bush shortly before Barack's inauguration. She presented the outgoing first lady with a leather-bound journal, inscribed with a quote from Louis L'Amour: "There will come a time when you believe everything is finished. Yet that will be the beginning." Accompanying the journal was another gift that seemed to embody the journal's quote: a pen, engraved with the date January 20, 2009. Michelle indicated this gift was to help Laura begin her memoirs. Her choice of present suggests that she carefully considered what to buy the former first lady; after all, although that date signified the end of the Bush family's time in the White House, it was the beginning of the rest of Laura Bush's life.

Michelle Obama has chosen other gifts as wisely. For example, she presented a delegation from the Republic of Ireland with a shamrock-green blanket made of merino wool. During the annual St. Patrick's Day lunch with the president, the group was presented with the hand-woven blanket, which was made on Swans Island in Northport, Maine, and contained a hand-printed tag stating it was "Custom Designed for Michelle Obama."[17]

With similar care, Michelle presented Carla Bruni-Sarkozy, France's first lady, with a Gibson Hummingbird acoustic guitar, one of the world's most iconic electric guitar designs, "as a sign of friendship," when the Obamas visited French President Nicolas Sarkozy and his wife at the Palais Rohan in Strasbourg, France.

Again, what a fitting present! Mrs. Bruni-Sarkozy, a former model, is a singer and songwriter. She has issued three albums and accompanies many of her songs on acoustic guitar. The Gibson hit the spot with Mrs. Bruni-Sarkozy. The two women really got on well and enjoyed a long lunch together, according to an announcement from Mrs. Obama's office.[18]

The word "gracious" was also used to describe Michelle by two writers, Katie Judd and Laura Lee Heinsohn, who communicated with the author. Katie met Michelle several times and was always struck by how strong, confident, and charismatic she is in person ("and TALL!" Katie wrote. "Like, basketball player tall"). Katie decided to get involved in politics and joined the board of the New Hampshire Young Democrats. She threw her hat in the ring very early for Obama, when many of her friends were supporting Hillary Clinton. Katie's whole heart was in Barack's campaign, and Michelle Obama was an important part of her ardor.

"She is a strong woman," Katie wrote. "Strong enough to know the difference between right and wrong, to put family first and ignore criticism in order to do what is best for the country. I met her at the NH Democratic Convention. I was nervous to ask her to sign something, but she was gracious and very down-to-earth. She signed my friend Garth and my convention passes, and Garth forgot to give her back her sharpie. She called him out and jokingly said 'Hey, don't you go running off with my marker!'

"Garth and I also hung out with Sasha and Malia for a bit while their Mom was working the room. They were playing school (we were in a classroom) and they were adorable."

Laura wrote, "Noticing many police cars, motorcycles, and the Barack motorcade parked at Lew's Dairy Freeze, I walked up to the take-out window and observed Barack and Michelle and their two daughters ordering chocolate ice cream sundaes. I was shocked at how tall she was; she towered above the secret service men.

"Barack began shaking hands with people. He walked up to me and shook my hand. I said, 'Yesterday I shook Bill Clinton's hand and today I am shaking yours; you're a lot better looking.'" The onlookers, media people, and Michelle started laughing. She was all smiles and seemed to be enjoying the little mini-circus. I was struck by the gentle interaction that Michelle had with Barack and her daughters; she was very gracious and sweet.

"Lew's brought an extra ice cream sundae. Barack turned around and asked me and the other people if we wanted the sundae. The lady next to me took it. He told her, 'Don't sell it on E-bay!'" Francina R. Harrison wrote, "I had the opportunity to hear and meet Michelle Obama when she came to Hampton Roads, Virginia to reach out to military spouses. I found her to be REAL, authentic and truly concerned about the military spouse/family. She impressed me as I was able to attend this intimate event for military spouses.

"I then had the pleasure of hearing her speak on the same night at a fundraiser. For some reason GOD granted me front seat spacing at both events. Of course, I got a famous Michelle Obama hug. Bottom-line, from women to women, mother-to-mother, black woman to black woman . . . I STILL remain in awe!" After attending President Barack Obama's inauguration on January 21, 2009, a Tuesday, Marva Edwards of Brockton, Massachusetts, was fortunate enough to meet first lady Michelle Obama at the White House the next day. "I had the most excellent day today," she said on Inauguration Day. "It was worth standing in the cold for ten hours waiting for the first family." Then, on Wednesday, she attended the open house at 1600 Pennsylvania Ave. "It was amazing especially after her busy day yesterday and last night," Edwards said in moving tones. "This wonderful woman found the time to greet guests."[19]

Michelle is an unapologetically proud black woman of style, substance, and the very finest academic credentials. She is a graceful, elegant, and highly educated individual of conscience. Great strides have been made in the public perception of African Americans, and Michelle Obama is helping to further improve the way African American women regard themselves. No longer are films and TV able to portray black women simply as maids, when the first lady of the land is a black woman. No longer is whiteness of skin considered the standard of beauty. Straightened hair may not remain de rigueur for long, when Sasha and Malia Obama sometimes wear corn rows and plaits.

Michelle is also helping to redefine the concept of female beauty for all women, not just women of color. Because of her, beauty is now seen as being physically fit and no longer as wearing size 2. Being beautiful is now viewed as a combination of warmth, intelligence, and self-confidence and of strength, attitude, and elegance.[20]

In her interview with Oprah Winfrey, Michelle defined who she is and what she feels she owes to Americans. She said, "I've always thought that what I owe the American people is to let them see who I am so there are no surprises. I don't want to be anyone but Michelle Obama. And I want people to know what they're getting."[21] Michelle Obama is a real person, open, and honest. The American people can do no better in a first lady. Despite her self-definition with Oprah, Michelle Obama describes herself primarily as "Mom-in-Chief." Although images abound of her on the White House swings with her daughters, walking the dog with them, and so on, when people in a Pew Research poll were asked to pick one word to describe Michelle, only 7 out of the 765 respondents used the word "mother." Instead, more people described Michelle as "classy."

So, how come Michelle's definition of herself as "Mom-in-Chief" isn't sticking? According to Carol Evans, CEO of Working Mother Media, "She is such a dynamic and powerful woman, that her being a mom is not popping out as her first trait." Perhaps, the poll results say less about Michelle Obama than about the age-old stereotype of mothers as supportive spouses who are content to remain behind-the-scenes players. E. Ann Kaplan, a cultural studies professor at Stony Brook University, says that this first lady plays second fiddle to no one, including her husband.[22] And, indeed, is there any reason she should? According to many polls, Michelle is now more popular than the president.

As if beauty, intelligence, gifts of character, and education are not enough for any one human being, Michelle Obama is also a creative person. For example, Michelle brought a piece of her Chicago with her to Washington when she had the fountains on the north and south lawns of the White House dyed green for St. Patrick's Day. Spokeswoman Katie McCormick Lelyveld stated that the first lady was inspired by her hometown's celebration of the holiday, where the city dyes the river green.

As writer Naomi Wolf has noted,

In one week, Michelle Obama sat for a formal White House portrait, dressed in somber, tailored clothes; posed for a snazzy *People* magazine cover, dressed in a slightly down-market, hot-pink lace outfit that showed plenty of skin; let the national media know that the First Family would be getting its new puppy from a rescue shelter; and had her press office mention casually that "secretaries and policymakers" had been invited for popcorn and movies at the White House. That same week, in the midst of the worst economic crisis since the 1930s, a national poll found that support for President Barack Obama was remarkably high, with respondents consistently saying he "cares about people like me."[23]

Wolf sees Michelle Obama's choice of clothing and activities and her down-to-earth demeanor as expressly intended to show that the Obamas are interested in democratizing the White House and the presidency. She thinks that Michelle Obama has paid attention to the example not only of Jacqueline Kennedy but of Princess Diana, famously dubbed after her death the "People's Princess" by the then British Prime Minister Tony Blair. Diana "told ordinary Britons that their world was as important as any other. She told them she wanted to know them, and wanted her sons to know them, too. . . . She taught leaders they would have to invite the people in—and treat them with basic respect—if they were to maintain their position."

Similarly, Michelle Obama's invitations to the White House "send out a message to the people of the United States. [her] guest list . . . says to the people, I respect you, whether you are rich or poor." It seems you can tell the nation more about your values by saying where you will seek a dog for your daughters than you can through reams of unread position papers. No matter who you are or how you rank in society, there is a place for you in White House thinking.[24]

Harold Clurman, that Broadway sage of the 20th century, said, "Deep thinkers of the theater who refuse to relate to its vulgar pleasures are off balance. They lack that essential ingredient of wisdom—the ordinary."[25] Surely, we can expand Clurman's concept of wisdom to include the philosophy of both Michelle Obama and Princess Diana, women as much in touch with the ordinary pleasures of life as the erudite.

Some people feel Mrs. Obama committed a faux pas when she, a commoner, touched Her Royal Highness Queen Elizabeth II. But, *The Telegraph*'s Clive Aslet thinks the two women established new heights of etiquette. He wrote that, in his opinion, anyone watching the television could not miss the chemistry of the moment. He described Prince Philip ducking in and out of the TV frame looking for a place to stand, as Michelle Obama had usurped his place by the Queen. (Michelle certainly has chutzpah!) Aslet said that the Queen seemed to be enjoying the situation, and revealed it with a gentle smile and a sparkle in her eyes.

The president and first lady visiting Queen Elizabeth II at Buckingham Palace, April 2009. (AP Photo/John Stillwell, File.)

When Australian Prime Minister Paul Keating dared to put his arm around the Queen in 1992, he was called the Lizard of Oz. But, when Michelle Obama committed a similar breach of royal etiquette and placed her hand on the hallowed royal back, the response was quite different. A small white-gloved hand crept around the first lady's waist, the royal arm too small to reach very far. The Queen apparently felt friendly toward Michelle, and for the first time in human memory, bent the rules. Her action was exactly right, and the warm, very human Michelle Obama responded in kind. The Queen's affectionate move was without precedent.[26]

It is remarkable that Michelle managed to penetrate the portals of Elizabeth's character. In the view of Michael Thornton of London's *Daily Mail*, the Queen "inherited the shy and aloof manner of her grandmother, the imposing, ramrod-straight, awe-inspiring Queen Mary," and from childhood on possessed a keen sense of her royal duties.[27] Perhaps this is the main reason she always has been reserved and standoffish with her subjects. It took someone as warm as Michelle

Obama to break through the Queen's reserve enough to enable her to put her arm around another woman.

Her move, nevertheless, may not have been motivated entirely by affection. Elizabeth II is an astute woman and must be aware of the epochal significance of Barack Obama's election to the U.S. presidency. Perhaps she learned from Princess Diana, after all, and in her own subtle way has communicated to her people that she, too, understands their needs and thinks of them as equals.

Despite their great class and age differences (the queen is 83 and Michelle 45), Queen Elizabeth and Michelle have become friends. On the last day of their sightseeing trip to the capital, the first lady and her daughters were given a private three-hour tour of Buckingham Palace and its 40 acres of gardens, including a meeting with the Queen. According to insiders, the two women have become confidantes after discovering that they have a number of interests in common, including the countryside, gardening, and clothing. They got along very well during the president's and Michelle's official visit to England, when the Queen was overheard telling Mrs. Obama, "Now we have met, would you please keep in touch?" Since then, they have exchanged letters and phone calls.[28]

First ladies often enjoy much higher approval ratings than their husbands, and the popularity for both of these figures tends to peak very early on in a presidency. During her husband's campaign, Republicans tried to portray Michelle Obama as someone who was vehemently anti-American, in an attempt to frighten voters away from Barack. Despite the fact that candidates' families are generally off-limits, Barack Obama's wife was besmirched on a daily basis. This tactic worked: in June 2008, a Gallup pole showed that she had an approval rating of just 43 percent, indicating that the negative portrayal of her had some effect on voters.

However, her public acclaim shot up around the election, and only two months after moving to the White House, her approval ratings were at an incredible 72 percent.

We don't have to wonder what changed peoples' opinion of her. Everyone got to see what she is really like as a person and were able to discount sordid right-wing talk. People had not known Michelle Obama before and could only base their opinion of her on biased reports. According to Robert J. Elisberg, writing in the *Huffington Post*, the change in public reaction was from "seeing her in action, seeing her grace, charm, intelligence, kindness and warmth—seeing someone who tells children in school, 'I liked getting A's . . . I thought there was nothing cooler than being smart.'" Exposed to the real person, Americans could see for themselves who Michelle Obama is, make up their own minds about her, and repudiate the brutal, destructive vilification of a lovely woman.[29]

But what is probably most characteristic of Michelle Obama is her love of service. The first lady told the Corporation for National and Community Service workers that community service is "the reason that I breathe." "It has become my life's work in so many ways," Michelle said, while visiting the federal agency as part of her listening tour. In an auditorium packed with employees, she told of a turning point in her professional life when it suddenly hit her that work as a powerful attorney wasn't the legacy she wished to leave behind her.

"When I thought about the things I cared about, the things I was passionate about, service was always in there," she said. With her customary sense of humor, the first lady said, "I could be some rich lawyer somewhere. If I'd stuck with that, I'd instead be writing checks to the Obama campaign."[30]

Yes, it does sound too good to be true that we have a first lady who, in addition to being gracious, generous, compassionate, brilliant, highly educated, and a wonderful role model for women of all ages, is creative and original in her thinking. But, in the opinion of the writer, in the case of Michelle Obama, the old adage simply doesn't hold.

NOTES

1. Harriet Cole, "Interview with Michelle Obama," *Ebony Magazine*, September 2008.

2. DeNeen L. Brown, "Michelle Obama Will Define Her First-Lady Role as She Goes," *Washington Post*, January 20, 2009, http://www.washing tonpost.com/wp-dyn/content/article/2009/01/19/AR2009011903139. html.

3. Ibid.

4. Rachel L. Swarns, "Michelle Obama Advises Anacostia Students," *New York Times*, March 19, 2009.

5. Lynn Sweet, "Michelle Obama Lets Students Peek Into Her World. Does She Do Her Own Makeup?" *Chicago Sun-Times*, March 20, 2009, http://blogs.suntimes.com/sweet/2009/03/michelle_obama_lets_students_p.html.

6. Ibid.

7. "On Their First Day in the White House, President and Mrs. Obama Greeted Visitors, Staff," *Associated Press*, January 21, 2009.

8. Brian Montopoli, "Poll: Favorable Rating for Michelle Obama," CBS *Political Hotsheet*, February 23, 2009.

9. "POTUS and FLOTUS Leave White House for Classroom," *ABC News*, February 3, 2009, http://blogs.abcnews.com/politicalpunch/2009/02/potus-and-flotu.html.

10. Rachel L. Swarns, "Could It Really Be Him? Yeah, Probably," *New York Times*, March 25, 2009, http://www.nytimes.com/2009/03/26/fashion/26washington.html.

11. Darlene Superville, "Michelle Obama Serves Lunch at Soup Kitchen," *Associated Press*, March 5, 2009.

12. Macklin Reid, "Martin Luther King Day Ceremony Is Monday at 3," Ridgefield Press.com, January 18, 2009.

13. Jeff Zeleny, "Q&A with Michelle Obama," *Chicago Tribune*, December 24, 2005.

14. Barack Obama, *The Audacity of Hope* (New York: Random House, 2006), 53.

15. Lonnae O'Neal Parker, "Defined by Her Times and Defining Them, Michelle Obama Is a First among First Ladies," *Washington Post*, January 20, 2009.

16. Tirdad Derakhshani, "Sideshow: Bo Has 'Star Quality,' Obama Says," *Philadelphia Inquirer*, April 15, 2009.

17. Walter Griffin, "First Lady Gives Maine Blanket to Irish," *Bangor Daily News*, March 25, 2009.

18. Peter Mikelbank and Karen Nickel Anhalt, "Michelle Obama Gives French First Lady a Gibson Guitar," *Huffington Post*, April 4, 2009.

19. Kyle Alspach, "Brockton Woman Attends Inauguration, Then Meets First Lady Michelle Obama at the White House," Enterprise News.com, January 22, 2009.

20. Dawn Turner Trice, "Michelle Obama Teaches London Girls that Brains Are Beautiful," ChicagoTribune.com, April 6, 2009.

21. Oprah Winfrey, "Oprah Talks to Michelle Obama," O magazine, April 2009.

22. Katie Connolly, "That's One Classy Mom," *Newsweek*, May 2, 2009.

23. Naomi Wolf, "Michelle Obama Is Poised, Clever, Savvy, Shrewd," DenverPost.com, March 22, 2009.

24. Ibid.

25. Terry Teachout, "Opinion Born of Experience, Harold Clurman," *Wall Street Journal*, April 3, 2009.

26. Clive Aslet, "Now That's a First Lady," Telegraph.co.uk, April 2, 2009; quoted in Tobin Harshaw, "Barack and Michelle's European Adventure," *New York Times*, April 3, 2009.

27. Michael Thornton, "One's New Best Friend: The Queen, Michelle, and the New Touchy-Feely Protocol," *Daily Mail*, April 3, 2009, quoted in Harshaw, "Barack and Michelle's European Adventure."

28. Andrew Alderson, "The Queen and Michelle Obama Forge Firm and Affectionate Friendship," Telegraph.co.uk, June 13, 2009.

29. Robert J. Elisberg, "Michelle Obama and the Hug. No, the Other Hug," *Huffington Post*, April 14, 2009.

30. Yunji de Nies, "Michelle Obama: Community Service 'Is the Reason That I Breathe,'" *ABC News*, May 12, 2009, http://blogs.abcnews.com/politicalpunch/2009/05/michelle-obam-2.html.

Chapter 8

THE OBAMA MARRIAGE

Anyone who saw them dance at the inauguration ball or has seen them look adoringly into each other's eyes knows that Michelle and Barack Obama are the Romeo and Juliet of the 21st century. Unlike many married people who go through the motions, the Obamas have a real love marriage.

Barack is not embarrassed to proclaim his love for his wife, no matter how many people are around. At his inauguration, the president said, "I would not be standing here tonight without the unyielding support of my best friend for the last 16 years . . . the rock of our family, the love of my life, the nation's next first lady . . . Michelle Obama."

"Not only does [Barack Obama] love his wife, he respects her," Kathlyn Hendricks said. "The model of harmony, shared humor and easy communication that the Obamas reveal really is a new model—if ordinary citizens practiced this each day, our world would transform very quickly in positive directions."[1]

Not only does the Obama marriage provide a model for a harmonious relationship, but Barack's love and respect for his wife may also help to inspire confidence and a positive self-image in other African American girls and women.

One sign in pop culture that blackness has indeed been main-streamed is the release of the Walt Disney Animation Studio's film, *The Princess and the Frog* (2009), starring Tiana, a beautiful African American princess—the first princess in a movie produced by Disney in more than 10 years and the only one ever to be black. Journalist Neely Tucker, writing in the *Washington Post*, draws a connection between Tiana's appearance and the arrival on the national stage of Michelle Obama, the nation's first lady, and the Obama daughters, Sasha and Malia, who are living out what seems to be a fairy tale come true.

In the film, Tiana spreads the word, in a manner Michelle herself couldn't have improved upon, that balance is the most important thing in life and women need both love and a career (not just a prince) to find true happiness.[2]

It wasn't easygoing for Michelle Obama during her husband's campaign for the presidency. She faced a storm of criticism after she made the comment that "for the first time in my adult lifetime, I'm really proud of my country" and spent the entire campaign trying to take it back. Republicans and Democratic rivals alike gleefully took her to task, including Cindy McCain, wife of the aspiring Republican presidential candidate, John McCain.

Other conservative commentators labeled her Barack Obama's "bitter half," while *Fox News* was chastised for slandering her with the racial epithet "Baby Mama." Nasty campaigns on the Internet referred to racist comments she insists she never made. No one has ever pro-duced evidence of these supposedly offensive remarks. Commentator Molly Levinson has observed that all indications point to the fact that Michelle Obama remains first and foremost true to herself. While ap-pearing on ABC's television program *The View*, she presented a picture of herself in sharp contrast to the caricature painted by her attack-ers. She talked about her background and her upbringing in humble circumstances on the South Side of Chicago. She told of attending Princeton University and Harvard Law School by virtue of hard work, and the high point of her life, in which she became a wife and mother.[3] True to herself again, Michelle addressed her tactless remark directly. "I think when I talked about it during my speech, what I was talk-ing about was having a part in the political process. People are just engaged in this election in a way that I haven't seen in a long time and I think everybody has agreed with that, that people are focused, they're coming out."[4] To the surprise of many people, including Michelle, her background turned out to be an electoral asset. Her upbringing on Chicago's black South Side and the common knowledge that she is a descendant of American slaves were an important rebuttal to early questions of African American voters about whether Barack Obama was black enough. In addition, her openness provided a neat counterpoint to Barack's frequently more guarded demeanor. Her biography also refuted Republican insinuations concerning Barack Obama's elitism. Michelle's modest upbringing with a blue-collar father in a one-bedroom apartment defies the charge that the Obamas are elite.

In addition, as Levinson noted, Michelle said on *The View* that she "wears her heart on her sleeve," as good a description as any of Michelle Obama, and also a nice contrast to Barack Obama. She is able to speak for her husband as no one else can. She has talked about what he was like as a younger man, the qualities she loves about him, and the reasons she thinks he would make a great president.[5]

Things weren't always so good for Michelle and Barack. There was a time when both were segregated and humiliated. When Barack was born, the short union of his parents would not even have been legal in some states. Despite her wonderful record at Princeton University, Michelle never felt accepted as an equal by white students. Nevertheless, we have come a long way since Rosa Parks refused to give up her seat in the reserved for whites section of the bus. Barack and Michelle Obama are the king and queen of a modern fairy tale that Shakespeare himself would have enjoyed.

Were they always so happy together or is that something they had to learn? Looking at excerpts from a 1996 interview with Barack and Michelle Obama (when the two were in their 30s) that were republished in the *New Yorker* magazine in 2009, one gets a glimpse of what they were like in their earlier years as a couple.

Although the interview took place only about a dozen years before, Barack Obama was not yet a state senator, let alone a U.S. senator or a candidate for the presidency. Nevertheless, he already had high hopes for his future. Even then, the Obamas talked about their marriage with great seriousness.

Barack said, "I'm extremely happy with her, and part of it has to do with the fact that she is at once completely familiar to me, so that I can be myself and she knows me very well and I trust her completely, but at the same time she is also a complete mystery to me in some ways."[6] Michelle was much more cautious than her husband. She was skeptical about his political ambitions, but was learning from him. Somehow, his flamboyant nature was able to bring out hidden parts of her personality.[7] The marriage, if anything, has deepened in the years that have passed since the interview. The partnership was powerful and unbreakable then, and remains so to the present day.

Despite his admission that he should take dancing lessons to avoid Michelle's teasing, the Obamas neither took lessons nor practiced for their first dance as the first couple.

"Michelle keeps on knocking my dancing in public in ways that have hurt my feelings," confessed the president, who is more sensitive to hurt feelings than he usually shows, "so I probably should practice just 'cause she'll tease me mercilessly if I step on her toes."[8] Obama has joked on numerous occasions that he won't argue with his wife's assertion that she is the better dancer. In an interview, Obama said that he was planning on doing a simple two step: "You know, nothing fancy."

Michelle and Barack Obama dancing at the Eastern Inaugural Ball in 2009. (AP Photo/Matt Rourke, File.)

Michelle also had some comments about her husband's view of the way she dresses. According to her, he doesn't miss a thing. She even refrains from wearing a favorite gray metallic belt in his presence. "Barack calls it my 'Star Trek' belt," Michelle said. "He doesn't understand fashion."

"He's always asking: 'Is that new? I haven't seen that before.' It's like, why don't you mind your own business? Solve world hunger. Get out of my closet."

She jokingly imitated him: "You didn't need any more shoes. The shoes you had on yesterday were fine. Why can't you just wear them for the rest of the presidency?"[9] Concerning the criticism she has received for telling the truth about her husband, she responded, "I think most people saw the humor of that. People understood this is how we all live in our marriages. And Barack is very much human. So let's not deify him, because what we do is we deify, and then we're ready to chop it down." She went on to say that the traditional wife's role is one of blind adoration, but her model is a bit different, as most real marriages are.[10] According to the British journalist Ben MacIntyre, "We're actually seeing an honest relationship take place."[11]

Nor is Michelle overawed by her husband's office. Barack often is seen intensely checking his e-mail on his BlackBerry. He was once observed checking the device at his daughter's soccer game, only to have Michelle Obama slap the hands of the president of the United States, thereby prodding him to put away his BlackBerry.

Despite all her teasing and making public of his flaws, Michelle told Oprah in their interview for Oprah's magazine that Barack has never disappointed her. She said, "Barack is a human being with flaws. And I can rattle down all the flaws and tease him about them every day, but those flaws are not fundamental. They don't hit upon things that are intolerable to me. In terms of his core values, he has never disappointed me. He is a very consistent person—which is why I knew unequivocally that he would be a phenomenal president. He is steady. Has he made me mad? Yes. Does he sometimes do things that I don't like? Absolutely. But as a human being, he has never disappointed. And I would hope he could say the same about me."[12]

The need for a strong partnership is deep. And they are able to drop in on each other when they want to.

Barack continues to grow in the role of husband and father. He said, "What I realize as I get older is that Michelle is less concerned about me giving her flowers than she is that I'm doing things that are hard for me—carving out time. That to her is proof, evidence that I'm thinking about her. She appreciates the flowers, but to her romance is that I'm actually paying attention to things that she cares about, and time is always an important factor."[13]

When asked in an ABC interview what kind of husband Barack is, Michelle said he "didn't pledge riches, only a life that would be interesting. On that promise he's delivered." She added solemnly that as part of their division of labor, Barack did the grocery shopping.[14]

At the beginning of his presidential campaign, Michelle was very frank about Barack's so-called deficiencies. She enlightened audiences as to how he just couldn't seem to pitch his dirty socks into the hamper (and he a basketball player!), that he leaves the butter out after breakfast, and is "so snore-y and stinky" when he wakes up in the morning that Malia and Sasha won't crawl into bed with him.[15] Michelle wanted his supporters to know that he was "a gifted man, but in the end just a man."

When asked about being present to his family, he answered, "It is important when I'm home to make sure that I'm present and I still forget stuff. As Michelle likes to say, 'You are a good man, but you are still a man.' I leave my socks around. I'll hang my pants on the door. I leave newspapers laying around. But she lets me know when I'm not acting right. After 14 years, she's trained me reasonably well."[16]

In her First Mates series, Melinda Henneberger observed that Michelle is more restrained about his flaws these days, perhaps because Maureen Dowd wrote that people "worried that her chiding was emasculating, casting her husband as an undisciplined child." But Michelle was not trying to sabotage Barack. She is a blunt-talking, authentic woman, who has spoken the truth as she sees it from childhood on. She thinks it is a mistake to deify anyone, which she felt Barack's supporters were doing. She doesn't believe anyone could live up to all the accolades being given Barack and was just trying to protect them (and him) from disillusionment.

"People think I'm trashing him," Michelle said to Susan Sher, her longtime friend and former boss at the University of Chicago Medical Center. "I was trying to make a larger point, that we want to put our president on a pedestal, when not only can no one fulfill all our fantasies, but we're all in this together, and we can't just leave it up to any one Decider."[17]

In a similar manner, both Barack and Michelle Obama have made a conscious effort to present their union as realistically as possible. Honest as they are, they may well have overstated the case, as they have made public facts that most political couples would gloss over, in describing their relationship in a "harsh bright light that makes you screw up your eyes."

They are practicing idealists in love, such as we rarely see, and function that way in a relationship rooted in equality. Decision by mutual consent is so essential to them that Michelle once took Barack along on a job interview to see if he approved of her boss.

According to Gil Troy, author of *Mr. and Mrs. President: From the Trumans to the Clintons* (2nd ed., 2000), "The Obama marriage is a modern partnership between equals; they are a working couple just like the Clintons. But, unlike the Clintons—and more like the Bushes— the Obamas appear to be a solid couple, devoted to each other, with no fidelity questions hovering overhead."[18]

Melinda Henneberger depicts Michelle Obama as a conscientious stickler yet a sane, undramatic type, who watches what she eats, regularly sees her trainer, gets enough sleep, and, consistent with the rest of her personality, overprepares for meetings. Until she became first lady, Michelle spent a lot of time at her daughters' school but was not the type of mother who hovered and fretted over inessentials. A former colleague characterizes Michelle as a person who "is not interested in massaging your ego," because she sees flattery not as a soothing compliment but as a trap that may cause trouble later on.

Both Obamas are pressured, Ivy League lawyers, Henneberger continued, but when compared to his wife, Barack is laid-back. According to Craig Robinson, Michelle's brother, "Barack has a calming effect on the family. My sister is very meticulous and straightforward and she's more of the taskmaster." Craig added, "They laugh more when he is around."[19] According to Jodi Kantor and Jeff Zeleny in the *New York Times*, Michelle "wants to keep her marriage 'sort of stress-free, free of the discussion, free of the analysis, free of the assessment.'" Barack's cool personality makes that easier to do.[20]

"My sister is really good at most things," Craig has said. "It's the way my parents raised us, that if you're really prepared, there's no reason you can't be good at whatever you choose."[21] Being prepared was one way to fend off the unforgiving realities of life on the South Side.

Barack Obama lacks nothing in the ego department, but he relies on his wife to keep it within bounds. She ensures that he holds the line between idealism and cynicism. In his books, he often seems to be writing for a single person, and that person is his wife. He is writing for her when, instead of glossing over the tensions in their marriage, he highlights his every transgression.

In a 2004 interview with the *Chicago Tribune*, Michelle said, "What I notice about men, all men, is their order is me, my family, God is in there somewhere, but 'me' is first. And for women, 'me' is fourth, and that's not healthy."[22]

When she is hard on him, it's not because she thinks he screws things up, but rather that she expects great accomplishments from him. "She thought he was so outstanding that if he became stuck in state politics, he'd never achieve greatness," said Dan Shoman, Obama's closest aide during his years in Springfield.[23] Michelle thought serving as state senator was beneath Barack.

When asked by *Ebony* in 2004 what she thought about Obama running for the U.S. senate, Michelle responded that she said to him, "I married you because you're cute and you're smart, but this is the dumbest thing you could have ever asked me to do." From her extreme cooperation during his campaigns, we safely can assume that she changed her mind.[24]

"She's his prod," said Denny Jacobs, a friend who served with Barack in the State Senate.[25]

Barack first met Michelle in 1988, after he finished his first year at Harvard Law School. Although he was nearly three years older than Michelle, their relationship began with an imbalance of power. He had taken a job for the summer at Sidley & Austin, where she was appointed his adviser.

"I remember that she was tall, almost my height in heels, and lovely, with a friendly, professional manner that matched her tailored suit and blouse," he wrote in *The Audacity of Hope*.[26] Barack immediately found

Michelle an eloquent beauty, but his feelings didn't become mutual right away.

When Barack took Michelle to hear him speak at an underprivileged area on the South Side where he had served as a community organizer before going to law school, she watched spellbound as he described "a world that could be" instead of the world "as it is." Michelle said, "What I saw in him on that day was authenticity and truth and principle. That's who I fell in love with."[27]

Their love is the most important aspect of Barack's life, the rock upon which he stands. If he had to choose between his family and his ambitions, he has no doubt which one he would choose. "If I ever thought this was ruining my family, I wouldn't do it," he said.[28]

Although Barack previously had other girlfriends, his relationship with Michelle was the first serious romance of his life. He felt he had been too immature to settle down before, but a change came over him as he entered his 30s, and he began to think about the value of a commitment that eventually would lead to marriage and a family.

With the extensive history of U.S. presidents conducting extramarital affairs, and all the temptations a president must face daily, does Michelle ever worry that her husband will be unfaithful to her? No, she doesn't. She says, "I never worry about things I can't affect, and with fidelity . . . that is between Barack and me, and if somebody can come between us, we didn't have much to begin with."[29]

Ever practical, Michelle prefers focusing on the present, rather than making elaborate plans for the future. "Our future," she said, "is making sure Barack can get to our daughters' ballet recitals and balancing the demands of this current set of responsibilities with our need to build a strong family, and that's taking a lot of energy out of us now."[30]

Michelle is a role model par excellence for everyone who wishes to have a well-functioning marriage. She keeps the books and the family's lists, and she defends values nobody else thinks about. "Michelle is the one who makes sure all the things that need to get done get done," says Cassandra Butts, Craig's Harvard law buddy. Every family should have a Michelle Obama, whether it's the husband or the wife.

NOTES

1. Vidya Rao, "Barack and Michelle: A More Perfect Union?" *Today*, November 29, 2008, http://today.msnbc.msn.com/id/27683815.

2. Neely Tucker, "A Fairy Tale Beginning," *Washington Post*, April 19, 2009.

3. Molly Levinson, "Michelle: Barack's Bitter or Better Half?" *BBC News*, June 24, 2008, http://news.bbc.co.uk/2/hi/americas/7470764.stm.

4. Ibid.

5. Ibid.

6. Interview by Marianna Cook conducted on May 26, 1996, republished in the *New Yorker*, January 19, 2009, http://www.newyorker.com/reporting/2009/01/19/090119fa_fact_cook.

7. Jake Tapper, "Asked What He Doesn't Like about Himself, President Obama Cites His Golf Game," *ABC News*, July 5, 2009.

8. "Michelle keeps on knocking . . . ," USA Today.com, January 15, 2009.

9. Maureen Dowd, "She's Not Buttering Him Up," *New York Times*, April 25, 2007.

10. Tonya Lewis Lee, "Your Next First Lady?" *Glamour*, September 2007.

11. Ben MacIntyre, interviewed by Elizabeth Lightfoot, *First Lady of Hope*, 2008.

12. Oprah Winfrey, "Oprah Talks to Michelle Obama," O magazine, April 2009.

13. Lynn Norment, "The Hottest Couple in America," *Ebony*, February 2007.

14. Melinda Henneberger, "The Obama Marriage: How Does It Work for Michelle Obama?" *Slate*, October 26, 2007.

15. Lee, Tonya Lewis, "Your Next First Lady?" *Glamour*, September 2007.

16. Norment, "The Hottest Couple in America."

17. Dowd, "She's Not Buttering Him Up."

18. Gil Troy, quoted in Rao, "Barack and Michelle: A More Perfect Union?"

19. Henneberger, "The Obama Marriage: How Does It Work for Michelle Obama?"

20. Jodi Kantor and Jeff Zeleny, "Michelle Obama Adds New Role to Balancing Act," *New York Times*, May 18, 2007.

21. Melinda Henneberger, "Inside the Obama Marriage," Slate.com, October 26, 2007.

22. Cassandra West, "Her Plan Went Awry, But Michelle Obama Doesn't Mind," *Chicago Tribune*, April 29, 2008.

23. Henneberger, "The Obama Marriage: How Does It Work for Michelle Obama?"

24. Joy Bennett Kinnon, "Michelle Obama: Not Just the Senator's Wife," *Ebony*, March 2006, 58.

25. Henneberger, "The Obama Marriage: How Does It Work for Michelle Obama?"

26. Barack Obama, *The Audacity of Hope* (New York: Random House, 2006), 328.

27. Peter Slevin, "Her Heart's in the Race," *Washington Post*, November 28, 2007.

28. Christi Parsons, Bruce Japsen, and Bob Secter, "Michelle Obama: He's Just a Man," *Chicago Tribune*, April 22, 2007, http://www.swamppolitics.com/news/politics/blog/2007/04/michelle_obama_hes_just_a_man.html.

29. Sandra Sobieraj Westfall, "The Obamas Get Personal," *People*, August 4, 2008, 57.

30. Kinnon, "Michelle Obama: Not Just the Senator's Wife."

Chapter 9

MICHELLE OBAMA IN THE WHITE HOUSE

What is it like living in the White House? According to Ronald Reagan, it is like an eight-star hotel. To Harry Truman, it was "the crown jewel of the federal prison system." For each president and their families, living in the White House has been an experience unlike any other.

At a meeting in France, Obama talked about the disadvantages of being president of the United States: "You know, it's very frustrating now. It used to be when I came to Europe that I could just wander down to a café, and sit and have some wine and watch people go by, and go into a little shop, and watch the sun go down. Now I'm in hotel rooms all the time and I have security around me all the time. And so just, you know, losing that ability to just take a walk, that is something that is frustrating."

And Michelle Obama? How does she feel about living in the White House? Unlike for her husband, it seems that she and the White House are a perfect fit. From all indications in many books and daily newspaper reports, she loves the place and was born to preside over it. At a "take your child to work" event, Michelle said, "I think I have the best job in the White House."[1]

The White House lifestyle also appears to be a good fit for Michelle. She and Barack have spoken of the strain his political ambitions placed on their marriage and how she resented raising their daughters alone. Things have improved for the Obamas since they entered the White House. The family now eats dinner together almost every evening, and Barack is usually home to kiss the girls good night. Michelle now seems much more relaxed than she did when Barack was campaigning. "She does look like she's enjoying it," says Stacy Cordery, who teaches history at Monmouth College and is the bibliographer for the National First Ladies' Library. "I'm sure she has been. First ladies who don't look like they're enjoying what they do don't get good press for their husbands."[2]

Above all, Michelle is her own person. She demonstrates this in every aspect of her life, but it is especially visible in her choice of clothing. Who else would dare to wear a cardigan while visiting the Queen of England? When photographing the first ladies, *Vogue* magazine usually picks out the clothing for the photo shoot: they chose a black velvet dress for Hillary Rodham Clinton and one of blue silk for Laura Bush. But Michelle Obama, bucking tradition yet again, refused to wear anything but her own choice of clothing. For her photograph on the March 2009 cover of *Vogue*, she wore a sleeveless magenta silk dress and used her own hair and makeup stylists.[3]

Michelle also controlled the way she looked on the covers of *O* magazine, *People, Essence,* and *More. Essence* editors suggested styles, colors, and accessories, but found Michelle uninterested. Similarly, editors at *More* were flabbergasted when Michelle arrived at a photo shoot wearing a different dress from the one they had agreed upon, although she ultimately was talked into returning to her first choice, a pink sheath designed by Maria Pinto. Michelle did not wish to wear anything but her own clothing for the October 2008 cover, and insisted on creating both the image and the cover, according to Lesley Jane Seymour, editor-in-chief.[4]

Michelle is shaping her public image in ways far more important than fashion. In interviews to women's magazines and the media, she has emphasized her domestic side: her self-designation as "Mom-in-Chief," her efforts to settle the Obamas in the White House and the children in their new school, her healthy lifestyle, and the way she has opened up the White House to ordinary citizens.[5] Michelle's passion for gardening is typical of her creativity and enthusiasm. For the first time since Eleanor Roosevelt was first lady, there is a vegetable garden on the White House lawn. Michelle began to plant the White House kitchen garden on the South Lawn of the White House in March as part of her wish to bring healthy food into their home and set an example to her compatriots. She hopes her efforts in planting vegetables, like tomatoes and spinach, on the 1,100-square-foot plot will encourage her countrymen to use locally grown food and induce them to eat in a healthier manner. Mrs. Obama knows "exactly what she wants to do," said Valerie Jarrett, senior adviser, confidante, and old friend of the president. She wants "to serve as a role model for disadvantaged youths and draw attention to issues she is passionate about, including education and the needs of military families."[6]

The aides who write her speeches select public events that emphasize the image she wishes to project. Michelle sticks closely to their scripted words, giving brief energetic speeches that rarely depart from prepared remarks, and (after her goof about finally being proud of America) avoid controversy. She frequently speaks of her support for volunteerism and her wish to improve the lives of military families, and rarely discusses race, her wish to influence public opinion, or her place as the first African American first lady in the U.S. history. Her frequent witty remarks, however, are all Michelle Obama.

At a luncheon prior to the 2008 election, Michelle told the audience her husband was "a great man, a wonderful man. But still a man." She went on to say, "I have some difficulty reconciling the two images I have of Barack Obama. There's Barack Obama the phenomenon. He's an amazing orator, *Harvard Law Review,* or whatever it was, law professor, best selling author, Grammy winner. And then there's the Barack Obama that lives with me in my house, and that guy's a little less impressive. For some reason this guy still can't manage to put the butter up when he makes toast, secure the bread so that it doesn't get stale, and his five-year-old is still better at making the bed than he is."[7]

A new dramatic public image has emerged since that time. She is now loved and admired for her warm heart, as can be seen in her trademark hugs and effervescent open manner. Her likeability ratings in the polls have soared higher than those of any new first lady since 1980,

Michelle and Barack Obama lead the way from the State Dining Room to the East Room after their February 2009 dinner with the state governors. (AP Photo/Haraz N. Ghanbari, File.)

and she is even better liked than her highly esteemed husband. Her amazing 84 percent approval in the *New York Times/CBS News* poll on April 27, 2009, significantly exceeded President Barack Obama's 68 percent.

In all likelihood, the change in public regard for Michelle has occurred because people now can see for themselves who she is, rather than viewing her through the eyes of her critics. David Axelrod, Obama's senior adviser, thinks the efforts of Camille Johnston, communications director, and Katie McCormick Lelyveld, the press secretary, also have helped to shape the public image of the first lady. Mr. Axelrod said, "I wouldn't say we're trying to soften her. But we want people to know her. There were caricatures of her during part of the campaign. Those interviews are valuable," he said, in speaking of Michelle's new persona. "They are important because they focus on her as a human being, which is important for people to know."[8]

Geoff Garin, a Democratic pollster, spoke similarly. "She's really opened up to the public, and the American people have embraced her. On a very human level, they relate to her as a great mom and as someone who is strong and smart and very caring."[9]

Michelle Obama is every bit the traditional first lady. Her activities, however commonplace they may be, rarely seem so because she usually adds her own original touches. The White House Easter Egg Roll, for instance, featured yoga classes and food demonstrations to emphasize healthy living, along with the customary egg roll.

According to Stacy Cordery, "Americans are happiest with a first lady who's a half generation behind. Michelle Obama has taken on the traditional role while giving it a modern twist. It's brilliant."[10] The image Mrs. Obama projects, however, does not do justice to the well-rounded person she is. As a graduate of Harvard Law School and former vice president of a hospital, she is a dyed-in-the-wool professional who cares deeply about public policy and occasionally recommends legislation in her speeches. Her important aides often conduct policy discussions in the White House that the media are unaware of. Her chief of staff attends the morning meetings headed by President Obama's chief of staff, and Michelle's policy director often joins the weekly briefings run by Obama's domestic policy adviser.[11]

The first lady's aides work with the president's domestic policy team in developing strategies to help working parents and had a hand in the selection of the chief executive of Corporation for National and Community Service, which oversees AmeriCorps, the national service agency.

Michelle feels so intensely about national service that she corralled a senior lawmaker at a White House event and pressured him to move more quickly on legislation designed to expand AmeriCorps. Her entreaty worked, and the president signed the legislation into law the next week.

Those who know Michelle Obama well often deplore that her intellectual side is relatively unknown to the public. Some blame the media for caring more for her exercise routines than what she thinks about important matters. Others are suspicious that the omission is an attempt to placate voters who prefer more traditional first ladies.

Whatever the reason, "We're not getting all of Michelle Obama, and that's a shame," said Connie Schultz, a journalist and author whose husband, Ohio Senator Sherrod Brown, is friendly with the president.

"But a lot of us are cheering her on and hoping we're going to hear more from that public policy side of Michelle Obama."[12]

A number of political analysts believe Michelle hopes her soaring popularity ultimately will allow her to speak more openly about policy, among them Paul Costello, an adviser to the former first lady, Rosalynn Carter. With such strong support, Mr. Costello believes Michelle eventually will feel confident enough to expand her boundaries.

Mr. Costello was indeed prophetic, and his prophesy has come about sooner than he expected. Being who she is, Michelle Obama already is beginning to change and to seek more power and impact on policy. As predicted, she was not satisfied for long with merely being the role model of the country. She wants to be more fully integrated into the West Wing of the White House. To begin that process, she changed her chief of staff from her contemporary, Jackie Norris, to Susan Sher, age 61, a close friend and former boss who Michelle believes is better qualified to get her and her team onto the West Wing's agenda. As an example of the way Sher works, she immediately informed senior adviser David Axelrod, "You need to get back to me right away when I call." It seems that Norris, 37, was "not on the first lady's wavelength," said a source who wishes to remain anonymous. "Susan is more of a peer."[13]

Further indicating her shift toward policymaking, in June 2009, Michelle announced the release of $851 million in grants for health-care facilities. Much of her husband's domestic policy during his first year in the White House centered around reforming nationwide access to health care, and Michelle's actions showed the nation that she was just as involved in the debate as senior policymakers.[14]

To help in her new stride forward, Michelle has hired a full-time speechwriter and advised her team to think strategically so that every event delivers a message. She doesn't want simply to show up and hug military families, but is determined to make progress. According to Camille Johnston, the communications chief, "It's about things that are coming up that we want to be a part of: child nutrition reauthorization act, prevention and wellness for health-care reform."[15]

Americans are fascinated by their first ladies. Because of their access to their husbands, they often are an important, if anonymous, part of the presidential advisory team. Their performances as the wives of presidents often mirror the changing roles of women in our society.

Most first ladies select specific projects that reflect their values, such as Jacqueline Kennedy's restoration of the White House, Lady Bird Johnson's program of highway beautification, Betty Ford's support of the Equal Rights Amendment for women as well as promoting awareness of breast cancer and the dangers of addiction, and Laura Bush's attack on illiteracy. Michelle Obama also has a project that reflects her core values—that of improving the lives of military families, which has become a personal mission of deeply emotional origin.

Although Michelle Obama was once a highly controversial figure, today the public's perception of her has changed drastically. She has become a superstar, with steadily increasing favorability ratings. This upsurge in popularity is partly a result of her reaching out to the military. "It's so counterintuitive of the notion that Democrats are antimilitary," historian Richard Norton Smith says. "What better way to display pride in your country than by honoring those who wear the uniform and who have suffered in the service of their country?"[16]

Michelle has been moved to tears by the stories of sacrifice on the part of military families, but these events are usually off-limits to the media, so the public has not viewed the first lady's empathic reactions. In addition, she invites military families to events in Washington, such as when an Iraq veteran and his wife joined her at an address President Obama gave in Congress.

When she met with two dozen military families in Fayetteville, North Carolina, Michelle started building a network of army spouses and relatives to keep her informed about the needs of military families. Michelle told the families, "As my husband, the president, said . . . in his address at Camp Lejeune, service doesn't end with the person wearing the uniform; the war doesn't end when a soldier returns home."[17]

At Fort Bragg, she spoke with military wives who told stories of having to use food stamps while their husbands were away on high-risk deployments. "That's not right or fair," Michelle said.[18]

The first lady realizes that not only do military wives have to juggle jobs and offspring on little money, but their spouses are often sent far from home and cannot help in the day-to-day intricacies of raising children. Michelle Obama understands the dilemma of such families, as she herself experienced many of the same problems during Barack's campaigns for senator and the presidency. She identifies with these women and knows from her own experience that they need all the support they can get.

Michelle spends a good deal of time as first lady in meeting with military wives and reports regularly to her husband about what she has learned. Thus, military families have a very potent advocate within the White House itself.

Michelle's demonstrated interests range from family and clothing to advocacy and health. She also makes good on her promises, such as functioning as Mom-in-Chief. She is a good mother and spent much time researching Washington schools to find the one best suited to her children. She put up a swing set on the White House lawn, got Malia and Sasha the puppy they were promised, planted a garden so her girls can eat healthier food, and returned early from her trip to Europe with the president to be with their children. Magazine covers feature the first lady with family members, and she is generous in giving her mother and mother-in-law the credit they deserve.

Journalist John Blake says that people who concentrate on Michelle's effect on Americans are underestimating her influence. The first lady inspires women of color around the globe, who can see themselves reflected in her and perhaps begin to see their own potential in new ways. In India, where having dark skin is considered ugly and women are thought of as cursed for having only daughters, Michelle is having a profound impact. "She walks next to her husband in public, not behind him. And she has two daughters. But no one calls her cursed," says Heather Ferreira, a program officer for an HIV-prevention program who works in Mumbai. "She could be a new face for India . . . she shows women that it's OK to have dark skin and to not have a son. She's quite real to us."[19]

Sue Mbaya believes that Michelle Obama inspires African women to take charge of their lives and become more assertive. In both their professional and private lives, African women are subservient and considered beneath men. "But Michelle is a high achiever who didn't intimidate her husband," Mbaya, a native of Zimbabwe and advocacy director for World Vision Africa, said. "I've always liked knowing that she was Barack Obama's supervisor when they first met. He once said he wouldn't be where he is without his wife. That really appeals to me."[20]

One would think so much adulation would go to her head, but Michelle explains what keeps her life in perspective. When she began to tell Malia and Sasha the details of her visit to the Queen, they broke into her soliloquy to tell her about their April Fool jokes at home. Her most important job, Michelle says, is to make sure her daughters, who will still be young when the Obamas leave the White House, are equipped for life beyond the bubble.[21] It doesn't look like she will have much to worry about in that regard.

Michelle manages to straddle both the domestic and the policy spheres in her role as first lady. Writer Autumn Stephens, author of *Feisty First Ladies*, remarked that Michelle Obama reminded her in some respects of former first lady Hillary Rodham Clinton. "But Hillary really downplayed the mom part, whereas Michelle has really played it up," Stephens says. "She's got the whole package. She's in a class by herself."[22]

To some, Michelle's chief asset is not playing some high-profile role, but by simply being herself: a wife and a mother and a clever educated woman. "She is the only first lady in anyone's memory who seems anything like the rest of us and our friends. She has a characteristic that can't be faked: she is normal. Women can sense normality 100 paces away, as well as in the pages of a high powered magazine. We know it when we see it."[23]

Despite the role she plays as Mom-in-Chief, Michelle Obama is not a traditional housewife. "Those days are probably over for good," says André Leon Talley. Instead, he likens Mrs. Obama to Eleanor Roosevelt, who was tireless in her quest for human rights. An early U.S. delegate to the United Nations, she was a first lady with no equal.

"She drove through the night to the very heart of Ku Klux Klan country to attend a civil rights rally," Talley attested. "And, of course, Eleanor served the nation, as does Mrs. Obama, in times of economic hardship. If Eleanor Roosevelt was a grandmother of the women's movement, Mrs. Obama is a daughter of it."[24]

Her assistance to African Americans and other people of color also is very new. Designers Jason Wu and Maria Pinto were catapulted to fame on Michelle's shoulders. Although she could have picked any school in London to speak to, she chose one with a minority student body. Although she could have been interviewed by Barbara Walters, it was

Oprah Winfrey she chose. Her appearances on the covers of African American–oriented publications have given a vital shot in the arm to black media.[25] In her fight against discrimination, Michelle most resembles Eleanor Roosevelt, the last first lady to take up the cause of African Americans, as she did those of youth and women. Because of the presence of the Obamas in the highest office in the land, the way African Americans look at themselves has shifted forever. All children now know there is equality for everyone.

One of the ways Michelle fights discrimination is by seeking diversity among all races in her activities. Few photos of her show her with anything but a diverse group. "Mrs. Obama's agenda has always been to include everyone and make sure the White House is open to all people," Katie McCormick Lelyveld, Michelle's press secretary, said. "We make a point at each event to make sure you see all types of faces of people with different types of stories."[26]

Michelle Obama is open, approachable, and down-to-earth with all kinds of people. To be a good wife, mother, daughter, daughter-in-law, and a first lady is quite a combination of qualities! After her great success with people all over the world, it seems inevitable that Michelle Obama will use her position and popularity to make a real difference in the cause of her choice, and go down in history as one of the great first ladies of all time.

Michelle Obama has big shoes to fill as America's first lady. Nancy Reagan said "Just say no to drugs." Barbara Bush and Laura Bush said yes to literacy. And Hillary Clinton tried in vain to create universal health-care coverage. But so far much more attention has been paid to the style of Michelle's clothing than to her ideals.

Michelle Obama got off to a fine start as first lady. Her first 100 days were just about flawless. She reached out to military families, served in soup kitchens, visited Washington public schools and health-care facilities, and invited children to the White House. "Mrs. Obama feels honored and privileged to be the first lady, and in the last few months she has been able to serve in a way that is authentic to her," an aide to Michelle Obama told FOXNews.com. "She is a working mother and wife and her priorities are family, community and service."[27]

The first lady of the United States has no predetermined functions or official job description, and perhaps that is why the role is full of unforeseen difficulties. Besides hosting White House social functions, first ladies must select the issues they will settle on, the agenda by which they ultimately will be defined. Every first lady has been criticized at some point for something she did or did not do, said or did not say, or what she wore, so we can expect that whatever issue Michelle Obama eventually chooses, she will be attacked by some group or other.

According to Debbie Walsh, director of the Center for American Women and Politics at Rutgers University, Obama typifies the evolving role of the first lady. "I think first ladies 50 or 60 years ago were lifelong helpmates," she said, a reflection of the era when women were expected to remain at home.[28] Betty Ford first transformed the role of first lady as an advocate for women's rights and health-care policies. After Gerald Ford's presidency, Mrs. Ford went public with her personal problems and endorsed aid to drug and alcohol abusers. Hillary Clinton redefined the role of first lady when she referred to herself as "co-president," and soon after President Bill Clinton took office, he appointed her to head the committee on health-care reform.

"Hillary Clinton is kind of a special case," said Myra Gutin, expert historian on first ladies and professor of communications at Rider University. "She was the only first lady to have an office in the West Wing," where she had 600 employees under her.[29] How special Clinton is has become clear with President Obama's appointment of her as Secretary of State.

Although Laura Bush did a great deal for the advancement of women, she took a less public route to arrive there. She first promoted her deep interest in literacy and championed women's causes; after September 11, 2001, she advocated for women's rights in Afghanistan and spoke out against human rights violations in Myanmar.

Every first lady must decide whether she will be active politically, like Hillary Clinton, or remain a traditional wife on the order of Bess Truman. Michelle Obama must confront the same decision, but she also is facing the comparison with Jackie Kennedy, one of the most glamorous first ladies of all time. As they did with Mrs. Kennedy, the media has focused more on Obama's style than on substance. On her trip to Europe to the G20 summit with her husband, what she wore and her convention-breaking arm around the Queen of England were given more media coverage than affairs of state.

"It offends me," said Carl Anthony, a historian at the National First Ladies' Library. "I think it's more endemic of a problem in our culture. It's eating dessert and thinking it's dinner."

Anthony said one of Obama's biggest challenges may well be to attract more interest in her substance. "She's a very powerful public speaker. If she were to get out and speak with heart and get behind a particular issue, I think the media will focus on her substantive elements, other than the style."[30]

"I personally am willing to cut her slack if she hasn't transformed the world for working families yet," said Debbie Walsh. "She's carving out a focus."[31]

Lady Bird Johnson fought for the beautification of cities and highways and conservation of natural resources for much of her adult life. As the first lady of Georgia, Rosalynn Carter already worked to improve mental health, while Nancy Reagan battled drug abuse while she was first lady of California. Gutin believes that Michelle will accomplish a great deal by working with military families, a project that also will enable her to avoid controversy. "It would seem not to carry a lot of political risk for her husband," Gutin added.[32]

If so, Michelle may have learned something from the experience of Barbara Bush. After five children were killed in a 1989 shootout in a Stockton, California, playground, Mrs. Bush declared that military-style assault weapons should be banned. President George H. W. Bush, however, opposed gun control, and Mrs. Bush soon made it clear that she would not make any further comments on the subject.[33]

Regardless of what Michelle may accomplish in the future, Gutin believes that so far the first lady is doing a great job. I haven't heard anyone disagree.

Allison Samuels writes that when first lady Michelle Obama unveiled the bronze bust of abolitionist Sojourner Truth at the U.S. Capitol, the moment was heavy with symbolism. Truth is the first African American woman to be honored with a statue in the Capitol. "It was the kind of scene I'd been hoping for when Barack Obama won the presidency last fall," Samuels says. "I knew that Michelle Obama was already changing the way we see ourselves as African American women. But I also hoped she would begin to knock down ugly stereotypes and educate people about American black culture. What's remarkable now . . . is how quickly and decisively Michelle has taken on the issues that matter most to us."[34]

In the early days of her husband's presidency, many incidents helped further ingratiate Michelle Obama with the American people. They were able to see her as not only an approachable and likable first lady, but also as a caring wife and mother. Sasha and Malia, despite their young ages, have always been well-behaved in public. Indeed, the whole first family was flawless on Inauguration Day, and since then, has shown no signs of letting their power get the best of them. Instead, they appear simply to be a happy family, who enjoy the moments they are able to spend together. When dolls of her daughters were proposed, Michelle Obama spoke out strongly in opposition, which showed the first lady's desire to have her family remain as normal as possible despite their sudden celebrity.

She has also stressed the importance of hosting state dinners and other events at the White House, as well as speaking to the public. She has helped make the presidency much more approachable. The Obama White House feels like a place where Americans can share in their lives, not an ivory tower where the elite run the country far from the view of the public.

Her fashion sense has also been highly praised, for ranging from "suburban-mom-friendly Gap to trendy designers and everything in between."

One of Mrs. Obama's greatest contributions is her "Let's Move" campaign, the fight against childhood obesity, which affects nearly one child in three in the United States. At the launching of the campaign on February 9, 2010, the first lady stressed its importance when she said, "The entire health and the future of the country is at stake." As a result of the efforts of Michelle and her staff to negotiate with restaurants and food vendors like Walmart and to propose regulations on nutritional content, considerable inroads on childhood obesity already have been made and the health of many American children improved.

Just as Hillary Clinton took her daughter Chelsea with her to Europe and Africa when Chelsea was on vacation from school, Michelle looks forward to traveling with her children during school breaks. "I've been grateful that my girls have been able to see parts of the country that I'm just seeing at the age of 44," she says. "It's not only seeing Paris, London, and Rome. It's also the remote places . . . exposing them to what we hope all kids will have: a feeling that they are citizens of the world." Michelle has already taken the children with her to visit Paris, where the kids gloried in visiting the Eiffel Tower, and London, and undoubtedly will escort them to many other countries before Barack leaves office.[35]

At the annual meeting of Corporate Voices for Working Families in 2009, First Lady Michelle Obama remarked that she knows the "challenges of being a working mother, and the feeling that one is never doing enough.

"I call myself a 120-percenter. If I'm not doing any job at 120 percent, I think I'm failing. So if you're trying to do that at home and at work, you find it very difficult and stressful and frustrating," she said.[36] During the speech, Obama urged sick leave for parents, more flexible working hours for employees, and on-site child care, which, she said, "is something that keeps many of us up at night. . . . You're just wondering where are we going to put our children where we feel like that they're being safe, that they're safe and being loved. That will relieve many of the stresses that parents feel on the job throughout the day."

Michelle said she understood the challenges of balancing work and family, "trying to do a good job at both—and always feeling like you're not quite living up to either—and trying not to pit one against the other, really trying to balance."[37]

Obama spoke about her own upbringing and having a mother who stayed home. "But things are very different today. One income really doesn't always cut it anymore," Obama said. "Twenty-two million working women don't have a single paid sick day. That means they lose money any time they have to stay home to take care of their kids."[38]

The first lady joked that in her current role she has more resources than most other working mothers. "Everyone should have a Chief of Staff and a set of personal assistants."[39] Yet, she was entirely serious about addressing the complex challenges confronting working mothers every day.

Not only is Michelle Obama comfortable in her own skin, but she makes the people around her comfortable, too. "The most extraordinary thing she does is she lets you be yourself," world famous photographer Annie Leibovitz told USmagazine.com at the Kennedy Center Spring Gala in Washington, D.C. "She wants you to be yourself, and there's no airs. It's great—she's smart, she's beautiful."

She added: "I've known them since the beginning—when [President Barack Obama] was still running for senate. What's so great is . . . we've worked with these people for a period of time, so it's almost like you feel more comfortable with them."[40]

NOTES

1. Lynn Sweet, "Michelle Obama's 100 Days, Nearly Flawless," Chicago Sun-Times.com, April 29, 2009.

2. Stacy St. Clair, "Michelle Obama Gives Fresh Twist to a Traditional Role," *Chicago Tribune*, May 3, 2009.

3. Rachel L. Swarns, "First Lady in Control of Building Her Image," *New York Times*, April 25, 2009.

4. Ibid.

5. St. Clair, "Michelle Obama Gives Fresh Twist to a Traditional Role."

6. Heidi Przybyla and Kim Chapman, "'Beloved Michelle Outshines Obama, Speaks to Youth," Bloomberg.com, April 30, 2009.

7. Maureen Dowd, "She's Not Buttering Him Up," *New York Times*, April 24, 2007.

8. Swarns, "First Lady in Control of Building Her Image."

9. Kenneth T. Walsh, "Michelle Obama Makes Military Families Her Mission," *U.S. News & World Report*, March 26, 2009.

10. St. Clair, "Michelle Obama Gives Fresh Twist to a Traditional Role."

11. Swarns, "First Lady in Control of Building Her Image."

12. Ibid.

13. Lois Romano, "A First Lady Who Demands Substance," *Washington Post*, June 25, 2009.

14. Office of the First Lady, "First Lady Michelle Obama Announces Release of $851 Million from Recovery Act to Upgrade & Expand Community Health Centers, To Serve More Patients," White House Press Release, June 29, 2009, http://www.whitehouse.gov/the_press_office/First-Lady-Michelle-Obama-Announces-Release-of-851-Million-from-Recovery-Act-to-Upgrade-and-Expand-Community-Health-Centers.

15. Ibid.

16. Walsh, "Michelle Obama Makes Military Families Her Mission."

17. Bryan Mims, Christi Lowe, and Stacey Cameron, "Military Families Share Concerns with First Lady," WRAL.com, March 12, 2009.

18. Walsh, "Michelle Obama Makes Military Families Her Mission."

19. Heather Ferreira, quoted in John Blake, "Why Michelle Obama Inspires Women around the Globe," CNN Politics.com, April 28, 2009.

20. Sue Mbaya, World Vision at Stand Up NYC 2010.

21. Mariella Frostrup, "Michelle Obama, Karl Marx and the Secrets of the G20 First Wives' Club," *The Guardian*, April 3, 2009.

22. Autumn Stephens, quoted in Blake, "Why Michelle Obama Inspires Women around the Globe."

23. Christine Louise Hohlbaum, "The Power of Slow: 101 Ways to Save Time in Our 24/7 World," quoted in Martha Irvine, *Associated Press*, March 17, 2009. OR Rachel Cook, "The Woman's Woman. Tough, Ambitious, Clever—and Very Normal, The Oberserver," Guardian.co.uk, May 3, 2009.

24. André Leon Talley, "Leading Lady," Vogue.com, April 11, 2011.

25. Stacy A. Cordery, "What About Michelle's First Hundred Days?" *History News Network*, April 26, 2009.

26. Allison Samuels, "Michelle Hits Her Stride: The First Lady's Diverse Approach to Diversity," *Newsweek*, May 2, 2009.

27. Stephen Clark, "First 100 Days: Michelle Obama Has Big Shoes to Fill, But So Far Is Walking in Stride," FOX News, April 28, 2009.

28. Ibid.

29. Ibid.

30. Ibid.

31. Ibid.

32. Ibid.

33. Clark, "First 100 Days: Michelle Obama Has Big Shoes to Fill, But So Far Is Walking in Stride"; Paula Chin, "In the Eye of the Storm," *People* magazine, October 1, 1990, 34.

34. Samuels, "Michelle Hits Her Stride: The First Lady's Diverse Approach to Diversity."

35. Talley, "Leading Lady."

36. Yunji de Nies, "Michelle Obama: The 120-Percenter," *ABC News*, May 7, 2009.

37. DeNeen L. Brown, "Work–Life Balance a Challenge, Says Michelle Obama, But Having White House Staff Helps," *Washington Post*, May 7, 2009.

38. de Nies, "Michelle Obama: The 120-Percenter."

39. Brown, "Work–Life Balance a Challenge, Says Michelle Obama, But Having White House Staff Helps."

40. André Leon Talley, "Michelle Obama Rocks New York; Liebovitz Talks About Shooting Her Vogue Cover," EURweb, May 7, 2009.

Chapter 10

MICHELLE AND BARACK AS PARENTS

Many special interest groups and media pundits continually monitor President Barack Obama's performance in delivering on his campaign pledges. In the early days of his presidency, perhaps none of those pledges created more commotion than the promise he and Michelle had made to their daughters to get them a dog if they moved into the White House. The way Michelle and Barack went about addressing the dog issue actually provided a revealing look at the Obamas as parents.

With the United States in an economic crisis and fighting multiple wars, it perhaps is strange that Americans and people all over the globe grew so obsessed about the question of the presidential puppy. Thoroughly examined in the media were the breed to be selected, the question of adoption versus purchase, the political consequences of their choice—and even what allergy medication would mostly likely ensure that Malia, who is allergic to dog dander, could live comfortably with a pet.

"Yes we can get a dog" shouted a headline in *Lab Business Week* about a medication for children with allergies. "Like Barack Obama, the inventor of Allergon Block is a father who was motivated by his desire to help his daughter who suffered from allergies." National Public Radio announced that according to experts, the Obamas were "setting a good example" in picking out a dog for their daughters. "They're doing all their homework; they're asking a lot of questions," David Frei of the Westminster Kennel Club said. "They are considering all the things that are important to them."[1]

In November 2008, Michelle Obama put her credibility on the chopping block in an interview on 60 Minutes when she said her daughters would have to wait awhile before their canine campaign promise is fulfilled. "Because as responsible owners, we—I don't think it would be good to get a dog in the midst of transition," Michelle said. "So, when we settle, get in a routine—we think about late winter, early spring—we're going to get a dog. Now, we cut that deal with our kids before America knew about it."[2] One must admire Michelle Obama for putting the welfare of her children before worrying about what people would think.

It probably is as good a thing for Barack Obama as for his children to have Bo around. President Harry S. Truman famously commented on the topic of dogs and the executive branch: "If you want a friend in Washington, get a dog." When Bo arrived, President Obama was heard to echo Truman's observation, saying "I finally got a friend." With all the complexities surrounding him at the present time, the president may well need a friend. Perhaps the most disputed part of the dog issue concerned adoption versus purchase and the relative advantages of owning a mixed breed or a pedigreed animal. When asked at a press conference what breed the Obamas might select for the future first dog, Obama spoke of adopting from a shelter, noting that a shelter was most likely to produce "a mutt like me." Some observers commented that the mixed heritage of a "mutt" might very well complicate the search for a hypoallergenic pet. Animal rights activists pressed the issue stridently, with shelters in Washington, D.C., issuing multiple invitations to the Obamas to visit their facilities and check out available and appropriate dogs.

In the end, the Obamas ended up with what Wayne Pacelle, chief executive officer of the Humane Society of the United States, called a "quasi-rescue dog." Bo, a purebred Portuguese Water Dog, was returned by his first owner to his breeder because he did not fit well into his first household. Yet, Bo never was relinquished to an animal shelter or

Michelle, Malia, Barack, and Sasha Obama keeping up with Bo, their energetic Portuguese Water Dog puppy, April 2009. (AP Photo/Ron Edmonds, File.)

dog rescue group. He came to the Obamas through Senator Edward M. Kennedy and his wife, Victoria, who were the owners of another Portuguese Water Dog from the same breeder. Learning of Bo's dilemma, the Kennedys sent the puppy to their own obedience trainer and then made a gift of Bo to the Obama daughters. Michelle Obama's spokesperson Katie McCormack Lelyveld announced the gift, saying that Bo's breed was a great advantage in terms of Malia's health concerns.[3] Bo is neutered, and in this respect the Obamas are in accord with the position advocated by animal rights activists.

It is noteworthy that Michelle's credibility score worked out just fine after Bo arrived and it became clear that she had been right about the timing.

CAN THE OBAMA GIRLS BE BROUGHT UP TO LIVE A NORMAL LIFE?

According to Sanford Kanter, history professor at San Jacinto Community College in Houston, children in previous administrations were not expected to be role models. They were required only to behave normally and not bring any shame upon the White House. "Good children from good homes in America have been the role models for the presidential children instead of the reverse," Kanter said. "The fame and goldfish-bowl life of presidential children is thus seen as a negative, and it becomes the duty of the president and spouse and the Secret Service to cocoon the children as much as possible."[4]

Obviously, it is not possible to ward off all public attention from the children of presidents, and the media are happy to feed a seemingly inexhaustible curiosity about their lives. "Since the last time there were younger kids in the White House, we have become a nation obsessed [with] celebrity kids right from birth," said the publisher and founding editor of *Girl Talk* magazine, Karen Bokram. "There has always been a fascination with presidential little ones, and they are what sells on the cover of [celebrity] magazines. Only someone who just died or Angelina [Jolie] sells better."

Malia and Sasha Obama are courteous, studious kids (as their mother and their father were before them) who set a fine example, and like most girls their age, they try hard to make their parents feel proud of them.

"The pressure to do well and make your parents proud is universal. It doesn't matter whether your dad is the postman or the president," Bokram continued. "But if these girls don't get straight A's, find a cure for cancer or play first chair in violin, we as a nation are going to be disappointed."[5]

Michelle Obama appears to be very conscious that her daughters, in their deportment and their dress, can set a stylish example for the nation's children, countervailing much of what children see on television and in movies and magazines. Nevertheless, in insisting on their privacy and generally allowing them to be themselves, she has shielded them from the pressures of being role models.

In attempting to arrange a normal family life for her children, Michelle Obama has decreed that her girls no longer will socialize with celebrities. The first lady is "trying to keep them grounded" and insists that the girls be given "no special treatment" in the White House. As a result, there must be "an end to hanging out with celebrities," according to family friends quoted by *US Weekly*. Michelle's priority as "Mom-in-Chief" is to make sure her daughters do well at Sidwell Friends School, a prestigious private academy. The family friends, whom the Obamas authorized to be quoted on the subject, added, "Michelle spent a lot of time talking to the girls about the new school and she's reached out to fellow parents at Sidwell."[6]

The media keep their eyes fixated on the Obama girls, perpetually watching to see how they develop and always ready to pounce on the first sign of misbehavior. Typically, the young children of presidents are kept hidden behind the four walls of the White House, under the ever-watchful scrutiny of Secret Service agents. Some presidential children who spent their formative years in the White House have not fared very well. While we cannot know the mental distress suffered in silence by some of them, we do know that the list includes unhappy people and eccentrics, as well as some who became celebrities. In some cases, the constant pressures and restrictions on these children have led to drug abuse and even entanglement with the law. People have a tendency to believe that presidential kids have everything, but growing up in the White House without being able to play freely with friends or to simply walk about town without being tailed by the Secret Service is often depressing. Let us fervently hope that Malia's and Sasha's wise parents will be able to prevent the girls from experiencing so disastrous an outcome to their father's presidency.

John F. Kennedy, Jr., Jacqueline and President John Kennedy's son, was born in the White House and as a young man was named "America's most eligible bachelor" by many magazines. John graduated from Brown University and earned his law degree from New York University. After he failed his first New York bar exam, the media inundated the nation with headlines screaming, "The Hunk Flunks!" Not a particularly talented lawyer, Kennedy managed to pass the bar exam after his third attempt. A decent man, John was perhaps coming into his own at the time of his tragic death at an early age in an airplane accident, in what many people regard as the Kennedy family curse.

The White House also has had its share of both ordinary and rebellious teenagers. President Theodore Roosevelt's daughter, Alice Roosevelt Longworth, was famous for her delightful personality, but at times also was an embarrassment to her father. Alice was known to smoke on the White House roof, was a gambler, and had late-night liaisons with men. She also kept a pet boa constrictor.[7]

What will the lives of President Obama's daughters, Sasha and Malia, be like? Their mother has said time and again that she will do everything possible to ensure that her children have a normal life. But can anyone, even the incomparable Michelle Obama, arrange that, when living under the glare of the White House?

The girls are now students at an illustrious private school and in all likelihood will attend prestigious universities. The lives they live already are far from those experienced by most American children. The president himself is a famous icon. We can only hope for a good life to come for Malia and Sasha Obama, as their father wends his way as president of a rocky country. In light of the wise and prudent upbringing they are receiving from the senior Obamas, however, it seems both girls have a better chance to achieve normality and happiness than most child occupants of the White House.

The highly successful first European tour of the president forged ahead in April 2009, but without the continued presence of the first lady. What a good mother Michelle is! She preferred looking after her daughters to being treated like royalty abroad. She flew back to the United States after overwhelming Europe as no first lady had done since Jacqueline Kennedy, leaving Prague in the afternoon and landing at Andrews Air Force Base early the next morning. White House officials said that Michelle wanted to return in time to help the kids start their school week, and that she felt she already had been away from them too long.[8]

Life being what it is, there invariably will be slipups, no matter how much care the Obamas take to prevent them. A photo of daughter Sasha in a blue bikini turned up on a photo agency's Web site, drawing many furious comments. But, in the White House, the girls are nurtured and well protected as much as possible, said Ann Stock, former White House social secretary during the Clinton administration.[9]

Stock is certain that Malia and Sasha can live a normal life, as Chelsea Clinton did in the White House. "I know it can work," Stock said. "Chelsea went to her ballet rehearsals. Then she came home, did homework, ate dinner with her parents, went to bed. You try very hard to make their lives be a childhood."[10]

The Obama children enjoy many activities normal for girls their age, such as dance classes, soccer, and sleepovers, and no doubt will continue to do in the White House. Also suggesting that a good future for his girls lies ahead, President Obama, who now lives over the store, has dinner with his family every night he is in Washington. And good father that he is, the president never misses a parent–teacher conference at the Sidwell Friends School.

According to former White House curator Betty Monkman, another White House child besides Chelsea Clinton who lived a normal life was Amy Carter, who in her White House years enjoyed many normal activities of childhood, such as playing in the tree house built for her by her father and carving Halloween pumpkins with friends.

"I think they had enjoyable lives," Monkman said about Amy and other White House children she knew during the 30 years she worked there. "Their families worked hard at it. Their fathers were there probably more than before. The media was not too invasive."[11]

Doug Wead, a former aide to President George H. W. Bush and author of *All the President's Children*, has a less optimistic opinion about the possible future of Malia and Sasha. In his book, he describes many difficulties White House children experienced later in their lives, including identity crises.

"Most White House children live in the shadow of the White House for the rest of their lives," Wead said. "For all their accomplishments, they are forever defined by something they said or did there."[12] As a result, many former White House children, such as Caroline Kennedy, Amy Carter, and Chelsea Clinton, often refuse to speak to the media.

While Malia and Sasha probably will not be left on the sidelines socially, it may pose another difficulty for them, according to Carol Weston, author of books for young girls and the advice columnist for *Girls' Life* magazine. "I don't think they'll get left out of anything," she said. "But you want to feel you're invited because you're you, not so your parents can get invited to the White House! In New York, we see this all the time with kids of regular old celebrities."

Weston predicts that the Obama family will successfully navigate the pitfalls of celebrity. "I truly believe the Obamas have laid a good foundation," she said. "You get a sense that there's a lot of love there, a lot of back and forth. Michelle says she wants to be mum-in-chief— how wonderful is that? And Barack Obama says 'I love you' to his kids right up there on the stage. That wins me over."[13]

Michelle contributed to the portrayal of Obama life in the White House as perfectly normal when she described herself as just another soccer mom. "I feel like I've never left Chicago. Soccer on Saturday—yes, I'm on a soccer field all day just like many of you. Slumber parties. We had about seven girls over, screaming and yelling. And we're shuttling kids back and forth to play dates, just like usual." Such wise parents seem to be keeping their children well adjusted to life in the White House. Michelle continued, "The girls are happy and healthy. They love their school. They're making friends. They're getting good grades."[14]

Barack Obama, more than any previous presidential candidate except John F. Kennedy, conducted his campaign with the help of his family. Michelle, of course, was invaluable to his success; and Malia and Sasha also contributed to their father's triumph. Whether waving at Barack from the stage, falling asleep on their mother's lap during his speeches, or worrying whether his half-hour infomercial would interfere with their beloved cartoons, the children charmed the nation and thus helped their father be elected president.

Of all the offspring of famous people, politicians' children seem to have the most difficult time of any. They are criticized mercilessly from nursery school on and are humiliated at the slightest indiscretion. When they do well, they are accused of receiving preferential treatment; if they are unsuccessful, as in the case of John F. Kennedy, Jr.'s law exams, the media rips them to shreds. The grandson of President Franklin Delano Roosevelt, Curtis Roosevelt, wrote in his memoirs of the ways his upbringing in the White House caused his self-confidence to collapse. At the advanced age of 78, he felt he still had not recovered from the damage.[15]

Malia and Sasha may be in for even more criticism, as they are female. Young girls are sensitive about their appearance, and the media seems to take great pleasure in critiquing the looks and behavior of politicians' daughters. Sarah Palin's teenage daughter Bristol got taken over the coals, and probably is still suffering from the onslaught. And John McCain told a joke about Chelsea Clinton so heartless and in such poor taste that the media, surprisingly enough, censored itself. At the moment, however, both girls appear to be adorable, beautifully brought up children, and it seems to this observer that it will be difficult for the media to find anything to criticize.

President Barack Obama nodded and sang along with a terrible performance at the "We Are One" concert, which was designed to welcome him to the presidency. As a gentleman and president of all the people, he had no choice but to appear to take pleasure in it. But his daughters didn't have to pretend to enjoy a dead awful concert. While President Obama nodded and sang along, his daughters behaved as expected for two children of their age. Malia's eyes glazed over as John Mellencamp, Will.I.Am, and Sheryl Crow performed, and Sasha fell asleep on her mother's lap. But it was another story altogether when Beyonce, Kal Penn, and Usher—artists the girls were more familiar with—took to the stage. They quickly perked up, and Malia enthusiastically took photos of the entertainers.[16] Malia and Sasha are being raised by a mother who is a top-of-the-ladder role model, and they have a fine relationship with a strong father. We look forward to seeing how these blessings will affect the girls' lives as adults.

THEIR CLOTHING

Michelle Obama dresses her children "in very classic looks with a trend to it, but not overly trendy," according to Suzanne Jones, owner of the Spring Flowers children's boutique in Palm Beach, Florida. Many other children's boutique owners believe along with Jones that a well-dressed little girl wears tailored clothing appropriate to her age, the formality of the occasion, and time of the year. Unfortunately, that is not the common approach to dressing young girls today, said Diane Inderlin, of Sweet Pea & Me in Palm Beach Gardens. "We see some funky stuff out there right now. A lot of girls are looking up to the Hannah Montana image, and I think that's where everything is going wrong. Girls have the rest of their life to be funky." Inderlin prefers "pretty" dresses, with or without smocking, and states that miniskirts for girls younger than 10 years of age are "out of the question." She also turns thumbs down on glittery clothing and leggings worn without a dress for young ladies. "It would be great," Inderlin said, "if girls begin to look to the Obamas for how they dress."[17]

According to Diane Levin, Wheelock College professor of education and coauthor of *So Sexy So Soon*, "There is a huge amount of pressure on girls to dress in certain ways by the time they are the age of Obama's daughters."[18] Malia and Sasha Obama demonstrate that children can be dressed stylishly in clothes that reflect contemporary trends while still dressing appropriately for their age.

BARACK OBAMA, THE LOVING FATHER

During his visit to Trinidad in April 2009 for the 5th Summit of the Americas, President Obama bought two powder-coated tenor steel-pans, one red, the other black, for his daughters.

According to Hilton Convention Services executive Vanessa Teel-ucksingh, Obama asked a staff member to buy the steelpans for him to take back home to Malia and Sasha. He did not want the pans to arrive after his return because the girls were expecting him to bring them presents, as he usually does when he is away from home. The president, who seems knowledgeable about steelpans, gave detailed instructions to his staff member concerning the size, tonal quality, and colors he wanted.[19]

With such a loving and intelligent father, it is difficult to see how Malia and Sasha will not turn out as well as he did, wherever they are raised.

To the surprise of everyone, the White House has had a calming influence on President Obama and his family, according to Michelle Obama, who says their new home has been a highly positive experience for her daughters. She told *Time* magazine, "It has been the greatest single benefit of this for us as a family. It means that we see each other every day. And that hasn't happened for most of the kids' lifetime."[20]

When Barack was Illinois's junior senator, Michelle was asked if she might move to Washington, D.C. Then, she said no. But, as stated before, now that her family has moved to the White House, she has found that she can enjoy Barack's increased presence at home.

"It's rare [for most families] to have dad at home for dinner, to see him in the mornings, to have him there when you go to bed at night, just to be able to have the casual conversations that happen about life at dinnertime," she said. "That's been terrific. It's normal. It's more normal than we've had for a very long time."

The president agreed with his wife. "I have got this pretty nice home office," he said, "and I am home for dinner every night just about that I'm in town. And I can read to the girls, and they can tell me about their day. I've even gotten to go to a couple of soccer games. We also happen to be blessed by two almost perfect children. So we are pretty lucky there."

When a child has two loving parents like the Obama girls, it doesn't seem to matter where they are raised. Mrs. Obama added, "We stay 100 percent in their world all the time. And I don't know if you understand that, but their lives are very disconnected from this [place]. You can do that with kids when they are young, because they just don't care."

The president agreed with his wife again. "Among the many wonderful things about being president," he said to *Time*, "the best is that I get to live above the office and see Michelle and the kids every day. I see them in the morning. We have dinner every night. It is the thing that sustains me."

Barack also takes work breaks he calls "Michelle time," when he leaves his office to visit his wife. Occasionally, Michelle will drop in to the West Wing with their dog Bo or the children for what *Time* calls "a brief but lively interruption."

"And if the kids really, really need to see him, they can," Michelle said. "They're free to walk in. They're welcome wherever they want to go around here."[21]

Lucky father! Lucky girls! Lucky nation!

NOTES

1. Penny Starr, "The Dog Days of the Obama Transition," CNSNews.com, January 2, 2009.

2. Sharon Theimer, "First Dog Bo Makes Himself at Home," *Washington Times*, April 26, 2009.

3. Sharon Theimer, "Promises, Promises: Is Obama Dog a Rescue or Not?," *Associated Press*, April 13, 2009.

4. Dahleen Glanton, "Pressure on Obama Daughters to Be Role Models," Chicago Tribune.com, January 14, 2009.

5. Ibid.

6. Vanessa Guerrero, "What Does the Future Hold for Obama's Daughters?" *College Media Network*, February 4, 2009.

7. Stacy A. Cordery, *Alice: Alice Roosevelt Longworth, from White House Princess to Washington Power Broker* (New York: Viking, 2007).

8. Michael D. Shear, "The Obama Presidency, Obama Abroad, Michelle Obama Returns Early to Washington," *The Washington Post*, April 6, 2009.

9. Jocelyn Noveck, "Obama Girls Facing Newfound Celebrity," *Seattle Times*, December 28, 2008.

10. Jocelyn Noveck, "How Normal Will Life Be for Obama's Famous Tweens?" *Associated Press*, December 28, 2008.

11. Ibid.

12. Ibid.

13. Ibid.

14. Sandra Sobieraj Westfall, "Sasha and Malia: Slacking Off on Puppy Duty?" *People*, April 30, 2009.

15. Curtis Roosevelt, *Too Close to the Sun: Growing Up in the Shadow of My Grandparents, Franklin and Eleanor* (New York: PublicAffairs, 2008).

16. Annika Harris, "America's New Presidential Music Critics," *Associated Press*, January 19, 2009.

17. Amy Royster, "How to Dress Like an Obama Girl; Mothers Feel Hopeful as 'Age-Appropriate' Little Ladies Take the Spotlight," *West Palm Beach Post*, January 25, 2009.

18. Amy Royster, "Dressing Their Age," *Palm Beach Post*, February 1, 2009.

19. "Obama Bought Steelpans for Daughters during T&T Visit," *Trinidad Express*, May 7, 2009.

20. Michael Scherer and Nancy Gibbs, "Interview with the First Lady," *Time*, May 21, 2009, http://www.time.com/time/politics/article/0,8599,1899741-5,00.html. Page no longer available.

21. Ibid.

Chapter 11

MALIA AND SASHA

Perhaps the ultimate claim to fame in the junior division of the pop-culture league is the Beanie Babies namesake dolls. After Barack Obama won the 2008 presidential election, the firm sold namesake dolls with the names Sweet Sasha and Marvelous Malia, until Michelle Obama, good mother that she is, exerted enough pressure to make the firm change the dolls' names. Company spokespeople said they just happened to like the names and the dolls were not named after the first daughters.[1] Yeah, sure!

"The nice thing is that, partly because of temperament, partly because of Michelle's unbelievable parenting skills, I've just got some happy, normal kids," Barack Obama has said. "And all that stuff that's going on around them, they just kind of miss. We have not seen any effects, any fishbowl effects, yet on them."[2]

Sasha is the youngest child to be brought up in the White House since JFK was President. She takes gymnastics while Malia studies dance, drama, and soccer, and both take piano and tap. Sasha is the spunkier of the two, often seizing the spotlight from even her father, while Malia is quieter and has an obvious love of reading.

Whatever the coming years will bring, it will help that President Obama has dinner with his family every night he is home and hangs out with the girls until they go to sleep at 8:30. He also arranges time to watch movies with them. In an interview for *Newsweek*, Obama said, "It turns out we got this nice theater on the ground floor of my house . . . So *Star Trek*, we saw this weekend, which I thought was good," he said, making the Vulcan hand salute. "Everybody was saying I was Spock, so I figured I should check it out."[3]

The president's solid familial foundation, with even his mother-in-law living in the White House, can only improve his performance as a world leader. But just in case he gets carried away with his own importance, his family will keep him on track.

The Obamas do not spoil their daughters. They get a dollar a week allowance and have to make their own beds, even though they live in the White House. The firm foundation Michelle and Barack are instilling in their children should help them survive the feverish years to come without too much difficulty.

Michelle, Barack, Malia, and Sasha Obama reading to children at the White House Easter Egg Roll in April 2009. (AP Photo/J. Scott Applewhite) (AP Photo/ Charles Dharapak, File.)

MALIA, THE CALM AND PEACEFUL OBAMA CHILD

Malia is indeed cool as well as beautiful, and has been since her birth, according to her father. She is aptly named. Malia is a Hawaiian name, and some sources cite the meaning as calm and peaceful. The name also is common in Kenya, where it means queen. She is also very beautiful (she resembles her father) and is wise beyond her years.

Barack and Michelle Obama are well known for their public displays of affection. Everyone seems to approve, including their older daughter. During their July 4, 2008, *Access Hollywood* interview, Michelle was asked about her last romantic experience. She answered that she raises Barack's children. "That is pretty romantic," he agreed. Then she added, "I think it's the little kisses . . . he likes to get attention. Just coming and sitting on his lap and telling him I'm proud of him." The precocious and prescient Malia said, "It also makes me feel good. Kids like it when their parents are all . . . except sometimes when you get to be a teenager and people think it's embarrassing. I like it though. It makes me feel good."[4]

According to Vivrant Thang, "Old soul Malia is wise enough to know that what her parents have is special."[5]

Yet Malia is a normal little girl, with the preferences of a normal child. Before Michelle gave her welcoming speech at the Democratic National Convention, her daughters were promised a surprise. "Is it the Jonas brothers?," Malia asked her mom. Apparently she was very disappointed when the surprise turned out to be merely her father's appearance on a video.

Sandra Quinn-Musgrove, author of *America's Royalty: All the President's Children*, thinks that Malia may be in for some difficult times before she leaves the White House. "Malia will almost be through her teens in eight years [assuming Obama serves two terms], and these are really tough years because she is going to have to mature with all their zits and everything else, not just before the country but before the world."[6]

The girls may well have to face all the usual adolescent woes, rebelliousness, new body images, mean classmates. But if Malia is as cool as her father thinks (and he should know), she will be able to handle it just fine.

Nevertheless, Obama is already worried about the time his daughters begin to date. He said to *Newsweek*, "Now, I worry about them when they're teenagers where, you know, you're already embarrassed about your parents and even more embarrassed on TV all the time." He's particularly concerned about when the girls start going out with boys.

"And dating I think will be an issue because I have men with guns surrounding them at all times," he said, laughing, "which I'm perfectly happy with, but they may feel differently about it."

The proud father added that he feels lucky the girls are so well adjusted, despite being thrust into the public eye.[7]

Malia already is admired and looked up to by her cohort, as they sense she is a special person. Every 10-year-old in the country wants to dress like her. The $110 red dress she wore on election night immediately sold out at Nordstrom's stores.

Malia also has a sense of history, remarkable in so young a child. She came back from her tour of the White House and said "You know, Daddy, I've got an idea," Obama told Barbara Walters. "You know how sometimes I have these, you know, big papers that I have to write? If I've got an important paper, a history paper, I think I'm going to go in that room where Abraham Lincoln, where there's that thing where he signed it?"

"You mean the Gettysburg Address?" Obama asked.

"Yeah. I'm going to sit at that desk because I'm thinking that will inspire big thoughts," she told her father.[8]

The children were afraid the White House wouldn't be friendly to kids, but their fears dissipated after their first visit. Malia was pleasantly surprised at how comfortable the White House turned to be. She said, "You know, I thought this was going to be an untouchable place. You know, the kind of place where you can't touch anything." But actually the White House is kind of homey, according to Malia's mother.[9]

Michelle has said that her children have adjusted surprisingly well to their new life. "They have been so steady and rock solid that I pinch myself sometimes. Sometimes I pinch them—*are you real?* . . . And that was always my concern: How are they going to do? How is this going to be for these little precious girls who were doing just fine in Chicago and had a happy life? But once I saw them thriving—not just living, but thriving, happy, excited about their day and very much focused on their world—that's when I was able to breathe."[10]

Like many children the world over, Indya Thomas of Newnan, Georgia, age 10, is thrilled to have the Obamas in the White House. She was particularly excited when she was cast to play the role of Malia in the Black History Month play at her church. Although the part is small, Indya diligently practiced walking back and forth across the stage and waving. "They're special because they are the first black girls to be in the White House," fifth-grader Indya said. "They are my age and it's kind of like me going to the White House."[11] Malia doesn't seem overly impressed by the fact that her father is president of the United States. While the Obama family was visiting the Lincoln Memorial, Malia, reading Lincoln's inaugural address, said to her daddy, "That's long. Will yours be that long?"

Obama answered, "Actually it's rather short. Mine may be even longer."

Malia said, "The first African American President: it better be good!"[12]

Even Malia found her father's rapid political rise astounding. While visiting Washington for his swearing-in after his 2004 Senate election, she asked if he intended to go for the presidency. Then she followed with a second question, very logical from a child's perspective: "Shouldn't you be vice president first?," she asked.[13]

"Are your children aware of the racial tension in your husband's candidacy?" Michelle Obama was asked. She responded, "My oldest, Malia is definitely aware of the significance of her father's candidacy, but mostly in the historical sense. She's aware that there was a time when both African Americans and women did not fully participate in society, and understands how special it is that both her father and Senator Clinton were competing for the nomination. More than anything, I'm so happy that my girls will grow up where the prospect of a woman or African American president is normal. And that's one of the major reasons why our family has invested so much into this campaign—I want them to grow up in a world where they don't have to limit themselves, where they can dream and achieve without ever hitting a glass ceiling."[14]

Both girls are following in their mother's fashionable footsteps. They wore adorable J.Crew outfits to their father's inauguration. "Malia . . . likes pleats and pared-down things and is not a huge fan of sparkles, but little Sasha loves bright colors and sparkly things," said Jenna Lyons, J.Crew's creative director.[15] It seems Malia's fashion tastes already lean toward the sophisticated, whereas younger Sasha likes to dress in a more fun-loving way.

When *Access Hollywood* went behind the scenes of the daily life of the Obama family, the girls were also interviewed. Malia clearly is turning out to be an intelligent, insightful, and extremely articulate young lady. She is obviously her father's daughter.

She is also unintimidated by technology. When the microphone appeared to be failing to work at the annual White House Easter Egg Roll, it was Malia, not her brilliant parents, who stepped up to test the mic.[16]

On *Access Hollywood,* the knowing Malia chastised her dad for shaking kids' hands. "You don't shake kids hands that much . . . you shake adults' hands," she scolded. In response to her dad asking what he should do instead, Malia said, "You just wave or say 'hi.'"[17] Things sure have changed since I was a child, when such a remark to a parent would have resulted in unpleasant consequences. In contrast, it is likely that Barack listened to his daughter and stopped shaking hands with kids.

In *The Audacity of Hope*, Barack Obama recounts a beautiful memory he had of Malia as an infant. "And for an instant, in the glow of the late afternoon, I thought I saw my older daughter as the woman she would become, as if with each step she were growing taller, her shape filling out, her long legs carrying her into a life of her own."[18]

In most of the articles published about the Obama children today, they are treated as one. Yet, young as they are, their personalities are quite different. Malia seems cooler, more intellectual, wise, precocious, insightful, and articulate. She is quieter than her sister and already has a deep love of reading. She seems perhaps more her father's daughter than does Sasha, who appears more playful and spunkier. Their differences show up even in their choice of clothing, with Malia the quieter, more subtle dresser, who dislikes "bell, whistles, and sparkles."

Malia may turn out to be even more of a fashion plate than her mother, according to Anna Wintaur, who says, "The jury may still be out on Michelle Obama's Election Night dress, but fashion critics and the nation's tweeners have been raving over daughter Malia Obama's ensemble."[19] Both girls are delightful, adorable, unspoiled children of whom any parent would be proud.

SASSY SASHA

Sasha charmed America at the Democratic National Convention in August 2008.

Michelle was doing a walk-through of the DNC stage to prepare for her welcoming speech. Sasha was standing next to her mother while technicians made the necessary adjustments. Suddenly, Sasha reached up on tiptoes and grabbed the gavel. She lifted it high above her head, brought it down hard on the podium, and cried out, "Order! Order!" The press corps broke out in laughter. *Huffington Post* reporter Seth Colter Walls said it was the "most recognizably human behavior" in an otherwise mundane morning. "Gotta love Sasha Obama. Something tells me she's the *entertainer* in the family."[20]

Then, following her mom's convention speech on August 25, Sasha seized the microphone during the family's exchange with papa Barack. When Barack told his wife she was "unbelievable," Sasha, who obviously thought her father was talking to her, said, "Thank you, Daddy."

Great as Michelle's speech was at the convention, her daughters stole the show. Both girls were adorable when they took the stage and wished their dad good night via satellite. Sasha blew him a kiss.

Michelle Obama told a story about Sasha to a group of students at a Washington, D.C., elementary school. She spoke about watching her younger daughter try to ride a bike up a hill. The more frustrated she became, the harder it got to keep riding. Obama told Sasha that the more energy she spent on being frustrated, the harder it would be to accomplish her goal. When Sasha stopped concentrating on her frustration, Obama said, she was able to ride up the hill.[21] Michelle told the story to drive home her message that students should keep trying and stay in school, no matter how frustrated they felt at times.

The Obamas make sure their children don't miss a thing just because their father is president of the United States. The president and his wife make sure to take a little time away from running the country to do things that are important to their daughters, like watching Sasha play basketball.[22]

In February 2009, President Obama also held down the fort to watch Sasha's and then Malia's soccer games while Michelle was away in California giving a speech. Call him Soccer Dad of the Year! The president yelled and clapped on the sidelines with other parents and spectators as Sasha's team scored a big goal. It appears that Sasha set up the goal. Her dad was very excited. Obama then moved on to watch daughter Malia's soccer match. Reporters were kept away from the game but were told that the president watched for about 15 minutes. Sasha wants to be like her daddy. Can you blame her? In a television interview earlier that month, Obama had said that Sasha had decided she wanted to join a basketball team. Basketball, of course, is her father's much-loved sport, which he plays whenever he gets the chance.[23]

Sasha Obama has been described as "The First Family Ham." She often steals the show. She has been in the public eye more than half her life. She is outgoing, funny, and confident, yet she is only in early grade school! She generally does adorable things and can be seen frequently mugging for the camera.

Always playful, Sasha loves to do gymnastics and tap dance. She also participates, like her sister, Malia, in piano and tennis. She is also a trendsetter: on her first day of school at Sidwell Friends, Sasha was spotted with an Uglydoll key chain hanging from her backpack. Shortly thereafter, Uglydolls were selling out of stores all over the district, while children hurried to copy the first daughter.[24]

On Inauguration Day, Sasha and her big sister Malia looked terrific but also like real kids. They will be great fun to watch in coming years.

Meanwhile, parents everywhere, take heart: even the Obamas have trouble getting their kids to keep all the promises they made when they were begging for a pet. "I got up at 5:15 a.m. in the morning to walk my puppy," First Lady Michelle Obama said of Bo, the Portuguese Water Dog, who joined the family on Easter weekend 2009, fulfilling President Obama's campaign promise to his daughters. "Even though the kids are supposed to do a lot of the work, I'm still up at 5:15 a.m. taking my dog out. So for everyone who has a child asking for a puppy—*you* have to want the dog," Mrs. Obama said to knowing laughter from a luncheon audience of congressional spouses. "As I do," she added. "I love my Bo."[25] Craig Robinson, Michelle's brother, says she is having no trouble adapting to the new first puppy. "My sister's always wanted a dog," he said. "She tried to blame it on the girls, but she's always wanted a dog." Since Marian Robinson never allowed pets in the house when Michelle and Craig were growing up, as she felt it would dirty it too much, we can understand why Michelle has always yearned for a dog and are happy for her that she finally has one. I guess as first lady, if she wants a dog, she should have one.

Someone has made a poster dated 2044, in which Sasha Obama and Chelsea Clinton are shown running for president. I wouldn't be a bit surprised!

NOTES

1. Rachel Weiner, "Sasha and Malia Dolls 'Inappropriate,' Michelle Obama Says," *Huffington Post*, January 29, 2009.

2. Jon Meacham, "A Highly Logical Approach," *Newsweek*, May 16, 2009, http://www.newsweek.com/2009/05/15/a-highly-logical-approach.html.

3. Ibid.

4. Maria Menounos, "Barack Obama and Family Chat with Maria Menounos," interview on *Access Hollywood*, July 7, 2008, http://www.accesshollywood.com/preview-access-exclusive-barack-obama-and-family-chat-with-maria-menounos_article_10226.

5. Vivrant Thang, "On Malia Obama Interview," *Daily News*, July 9, 2008.

6. Dahleen Glanton, "Pressure on Obama Daughters to Be Role Models," *Chicago Tribune*, January 14, 2009.

7. Meacham, "A Highly Logical Approach."

8. Barbara Walters, "A Barbara Walters Special: Barack and Michelle Obama," Interview on *ABC News*, November 26, 2008, http://abcnews.go.com/Politics/President44/story?id=6342700&page=1.

9. Ibid.

10. Oprah Winfrey, "Oprah Talks with Michelle Obama," O magazine, April 2009.

11. Glanton, "Pressure on Obama Daughters to Be Role Models."

12. Anne E. Kornblut, "D.C. Vote on Obama's Agenda, But Low," *Washington Post*, January 16, 2009.

13. "NYT Chronicles Obama's Historic Journey," excerpts from "Obama, The Historic Journey," MSNBC, February 16, 2009, http://today.msnbc.msn.com/id/29221720.

14. Michelle Obama, "Michelle Obama on Hannah Montana and Toned Arms," interview with Momlogic Online magazine, July 31, 2008, http://www.momlogic.com/2008/07/20_questions_with_michelle_oba.php.

15. Cheryl Lu-Lien Tan, "J.Crew's Continuing Obama Moment," *Wall Street Journal*, January 22, 2009, http://blogs.wsj.com/runway/2009/01/22/jcrews-continuing-obama-moment/.

16. Karen Travers, "Obamas Open White House for Annual Easter Egg Roll," *ABC News*, April 13, 2009, http://abcnews.go.com/Politics/story?id=7306401&page=1.

17. Menounos, "Barack Obama and Family Chat with Maria Menounos."

18. Barack Obama, *The Audacity of Hope* (New York: Random House, 2006).

19. Anna Wintaur, quoted in "Malia Obama's Election Night Dress in Demand," at *Thoughts for an Industry Chic*, November 11, 2008, http://blog.kainoainc.com/entertainment-tidbits/et-111208/.

20. Stuart Whatley, "Obama's Daughter on Inaugural Speech," *Huffington Post*, January 16, 2009.

21. Lynn Sweet, "Michelle Obama's Advice for Bad Days," Politicsdaily.com, May 14, 2009, http://www.politicsdaily.com/2009/05/14/michelle-obamas-advice-for-bad-days/.

22. Associated Press, "Obamas Take a Break for Sasha's Basketball Game," *Today*, February 21, 2009, http://today.msnbc.msn.com/id/29319056.

23. Nick Graham, "Sasha, Malia Cheered on by Soccer Dad Obama," *Huffington Post*, May 16, 2009, http://www.huffingtonpost.com/2009/05/16/obama-soccer-photos-sasha_n_204278.html.

24. Kathleen Parker, "How Sasha Obama Triggered a Hot Washington Fad," *Daily Beast*, January 14, 2009, http://www.thedailybeast.com/blogs-and-stories/2009-01-14/how-sasha-obama-triggered-a-hot-washington-fad/#.

25. Michelle Obama, "Remarks by the First Lady at a Congressional Club Luncheon," April 30, 2009, http://www.whitehouse.gov/the-press-office/remarks-first-lady-a-congressional-club-luncheon.

Chapter 12

MICHELLE OBAMA, FIRST LADY OF FASHION

Designers have been mad about Michelle Obama ever since her appearance at the 2008 Democratic Convention. She is their dream come true. They have been waiting for her like the Second Coming (Jackie Kennedy, of course, is the first), for what Maria Puente tells us is a "real woman with a real body who can inspire fashionable apparel aimed at middle-aged women overlooked by a youth-obsessed industry." Retailers such as J.Crew, Liz Claiborne, Talbot, and Saks Fifth Avenue, says Puente, are confident that the first lady's enthusiasm will continue to sell apparel like "Elie Tahari's $598 purple-floral sheath 'Michelle' dress."[1]

The *Wall Street Journal* agrees, stating that designers are now looking at Michelle Obama as their style muse and an exemplary setter of fashion trends.[2]

The fashion daily *WWD* remarked, "The American fashion industry hasn't had a catch this big since, well, since another icon of Democratic chic took up residency on Pennsylvania Avenue in 1961."[3]

But, despite the frequent comparison to Jacqueline Kennedy, Michelle is no copycat. Puente notes that she sports her own look in striking colors, such as tomato red, lemony yellow, shimmering violet, and bright turquoise. With her fit body and graceful height, she looks as elegant in a white shirt, pants, and low heels or an off-the-rack print sheath as in a designer creation. Still, she is partial to dresses and often goes sleeveless. With those arms, who can blame her?

According to fashion editor Bonnie Fuller, Michelle has preferred wearing dresses ever since she was criticized for seeming too strong.

"There's something about a woman in a suit that American men and women still find intimidating. A suit strikes them as too cold, too impersonal and too ambitious," Bonnie Fuller writes.[4]

The author of *Michelle Style*, Mandi Norwood, calls Michelle "The First Lady of Fashion." Norwood believes the fashion industry has been waiting for just such a first lady for many years.

"First ladies tend to be unfairly judged by what they wear, so appearance is almost as important as what she says," Norwood continues. "Michelle has her own style, but it's not contrived, it feels incredibly natural. That's why she has been so universally accepted as a fashion icon. . . . Mrs. Obama has taken that style we admire and given it a lovely playful twist that's not so aristocratic and is much more relatable."[5]

Michelle has been named to *Vanity Fair*'s International Best-Dressed list, as a reward for her "independent and strong and distinct fashion sense." There's even a Web site (www.mrs-o.org) that notes every change in her wardrobe.

The fashion of recent presidential wives has varied greatly, from Nancy Reagan's love of designer clothing to Hillary Clinton's infamous pantsuits. "It's rare to have a woman in that position who feels and looks like a real person," says designer Sigrid Olsen, speaking of Michelle Obama. "She's modern-looking, she's fit, and she seems to be able to wear clothes with a sense of style. Women these days are looking for a way to dress appropriately and tastefully and not look frumpy. She's able to do that, and she looks very comfortable in her own skin."[6]

Most first ladies, except for Jacqueline Kennedy, have been pretty old fashioned, Olsen says. "They've worn very conservative, traditional clothing. Obama shows you can be classic and tasteful without having to be too conservative and still make a statement. She represents most women's idea of what fashion is."[7]

Felix Mercado, fashion stylist and president of www.sayitwithstyle. com, finds it very exciting to see so much interest paid to the first lady's wardrobe. "The fact she likes to dress won't diminish her role," he says. "She has a big influence on the fashion scene. She wears designer labels, but she also shops at department stores. She was doing the recessionista thing before we went into a recession."[8]

Michelle likes bold prints and patterns that accentuate her curves and full 5 foot 11 inches. And bare legs! Our unconventional first lady says she doesn't wear pantyhose because her height makes wearing them uncomfortable.

She also has a gift for selecting unusual accessories. She might clip a feather brooch onto the neckline of a dress, wear a necklace made of pearls the size of gumballs, or tightly encircle her waist with a slender studded belt.

In a recession that has dug in its heels, women are delighted to see Michelle wearing the creations of young designers, such as Thakoon and Maria Pinto, and shopping in J.Crew and Target.

What Michelle Obama wears, women all over the country suddenly want. When she sported a leaf-print dress on the television program *The View* that cost $148, Donna Ricco's creation sold out almost immediately. And when Michelle announced on the *Tonight Show with Jay Leno* that she had bought her outfit from J.Crew online, it, too, disappeared from the shelves.

"She's really tapped into the fashion mood of the moment," Jacqui Stafford, executive style editor of *Shape* magazine, says. "She proves you can look stylish dressing in pieces from across every breadth of the fashion spectrum. And as a political statement, she's telling women, 'Look, I'm just like you.'"[9]

Being human, even Michelle can have a bad clothes night. The black and red Narciso Rodriguez dress she wore on election night irritated many. "Disastrous frock!" critics griped, and they compared the dress to a Halloween costume and said it had a "lava lamp look."

Lesley Jane Seymour, editor of *More* magazine, says, "Obama has a look and style that she cultivates carefully and is not going to let anyone, including fashion editors from New York, tell her what to do. In a world where most personal style is relentlessly boring and uninspiring . . . it's refreshing, if not always convenient, to see Obama cutting her own cloth."[10]

Just how much she controls her wardrobe was evident when Michelle refused to wear the designer clothing provided her for the shoot for

More. Instead, she chose to wear a sheath of her own, created by Maria Pinto.

Michelle is doing her best to get used to all the commotion about her wardrobe. "It's hard," she said to *ABC News*. "I'm kind of a tomboy jock at heart, but I like to look nice."[11]

Fashion gurus are passionately interested in the wife of the president, and they believe Michelle is using her position as first lady to rescue a shaky industry. Steven Kolb, executive director of the Council of Fashion Designers, says American fashion needs a big shot in the arm now.[12] And, apparently, that is exactly what it is getting from the talented Michelle Obama.

Summing up Michelle Obama's style, the *New York Times*'s Guy Trebay writes that Michelle Obama took a bold and unprecedented action during her husband's campaign for the presidency, in which she demonstrated her interest both in looking stylish and furthering American fashion and its designers. Her cosmopolitan approach serves as an example to all women who wish to be well dressed without breaking the bank. She is self-confident enough to alter dress details herself in her sincere belief that "it is the woman who should wear the clothes and not the other way around." "My perception is that she's already had an extremely potent effect on the business," Hamish Bowles, *Vogue* editor and curator of *Jacqueline Kennedy: The White House Years*, was quoted in the *New York Times* as saying.

Said Stephanie Solomon, Bloomingdale's fashion director, "There is something timely about celebrating American fashion and American designers. Mrs. Obama is, first of all, very elegant and has wonderful taste. But she also recognizes the value of beautiful dresses and not big prices. Michelle Obama came into the limelight with her good sense of dressing observed throughout the campaign, giving out the message that clothes portray the individuality of the person."[13]

One cannot speak of Michelle Obama's style without taking her person into account. "It is her height, the way she carries herself, the tone and tenor of conversation she has with people and the way she enunciates her words. She just seems like a very strong woman," said Michelle Bernard of the Independent Women's Forum.[14]

Author and professor Stacy A. Cordery notes of Michelle Obama that "if her topics have been traditional, her fashion sense has not. While this matters greatly to the couture world, to clothes-conscious

Americans, and to African American women . . . it is most important to the Obama administration" because her appearances before the public are swamped by the media. They make frequent references to Jacqueline Kennedy, who, like Michelle Obama, was "beautiful, young, charming, photogenic, and talented." The styles worn by both women are a drastic departure from those of previous first ladies. Fashion has long been associated with first ladies, whose eye-catching creations bring attention from the media. Michelle's dramatic, unique choices suggest hope and change.[15]

The curator of the Smithsonian's First Ladies Collection tells us first ladies' gowns traditionally mirror the times in a very sophisticated way.

With a *Mad Men*–era silhouette and color of the moment—bright yellow—Isabel Toledo's Inauguration Day ensemble shows that Michelle Obama is able to strike a balance between the old and the new. Although some people think the beaded collar on her inaugural

Inauguration day: a frigid January 20, 2009. Michelle and Barack Obama walk up Pennsylvania Avenue toward the White House. Michelle wore an ensemble by Isabel Toledo. (AP Photo/Doug Mills, Pool.)

dress was too formal for morning, the rules have changed. Today, it startles no one to see a guest wearing black to a wedding or a white dress at night.

By wearing clothes from youthful stylists, Michelle is extending a helping hand to a new generation of talent and opening doors to a state-of-the-art era of fashion. For example, she wore a creamy one-shouldered gown by the Taiwanese American designer Jason Wu to the inaugural balls.

"You're going to choose something that you like, something that you're comfortable in, something you think is appropriate, but also something you think is going to be pretty. You know all eyes gonna be on you. These photos will follow you to the grave," says curator Lisa Kathleen Graddy.[16]

Michelle Obama also changed the rules on inauguration night by wearing a highly unusual gown to the various inaugural balls—one that would have made a beautiful wedding dress. The president, who un-doubtedly took a page from his wife's book, wearing a white bow tie and tux combination, made an elegant escort for the stunning first lady.

During the inaugural events, Michelle wore a number of shoulder-length diamond earrings created by jeweler Loree Rodkin. They were on loan from Ikram, her favorite Chicago boutique. While Nancy Reagan was reprimanded publicly for borrowing clothes, times have changed, and the lending of their creations is now an important form of advertising for designers.

First Lady Michelle Obama's style statement will inspire more eth-nic and class differences in fashions, according to New Hampshire so-ciologist and fashion expert Catherine Moran. Michelle's choices in clothing often indicate that she is aware of and interested in foreign designs. Moran brought out that Michelle's wardrobe emphasizes the "structure of diversity, in particular the heterogeneity of ethnic groups and social standing. Her election night dress was designed by Narciso Rodriguez, the son of Cuban immigrants."[17]

On the evening of her husband's acceptance speech as the Demo-cratic candidate, Michelle once again made an ethnic statement when she wore a design by Thai-born designer Thakoon Panichgul.

After almost 50 years, we finally have a first lady who is able to claim the title of first lady of fashion held by Jacqueline Kennedy. The two

have many similarities, both young, modern women who have capti-
vated the hearts of the American people. As such, *Badger Herald* journalist Jessica Gressa can understand very well why Michelle is labeled a
fashion icon. Gressa adores Michelle Obama both as a woman and first
lady, and believes she is "stunning, supportive and an incredibly optimistic symbol for our country." Nevertheless, despite her unadulterated
admiration for Michelle Obama, Gressa does not believe that Michelle
"always hits the mark or displays the same sophistication that would
grant her the title of 'icon.'"[18]

Despite the insistence of many leaders of the fashion community
that she is this generation's Jacqueline Kennedy, Michelle Obama's
approach to fashion actually is quite different. Fifty years ago, Jackie
Kennedy set out to show the world that despite its reputation of being
a rustic, uncultured country, United States was a nation of elegance,
poise, and culture. Mrs. Kennedy presented herself and her husband
as children of privilege, America's king and queen. Kennedy's self-
representation was in great contrast to Michelle's; Michelle continually stresses her background as a middle-class child of the South Side
of Chicago.

Gressa thinks that Obama cannot be recognized as a fashion icon
like Jacqueline Kennedy because she does not in any way attempt to be
one. She is not a person who has close relationships with the designers,
nor has she studied art or design. She herself claims that she just wears
what she likes. Therefore, Gressa believes that, although Michelle
Obama is young and has brought about a change in what women wear
and admire in clothes, she is not a match for the chic style of a fashion
icon. Michelle should be lauded for her intelligence, confidence, and
generosity, and is a symbol of the optimism and change that is sweeping
the nation—but not for fashion.[19]

Nevertheless, despite Gressa's opinion, and the fact that Michelle
Obama clearly has her own unique sense of style, it seems that fashion
experts can't resist comparing her to Mrs. Kennedy.

A few people are even harder on Michelle than Gressa. In April
2009, Michelle Obama visited London dressed in a riot of color. She
sported dark, slim-fitting trousers with a transparent tunic trimmed
with large rows of yellow, orange, and purple pastel flower designs and
topped with not one, but two layer cardigans in blue and yellow. On

a trip to Westminster Abbey with her daughters, Michelle pulled her outfit together with a polka dot belt with a purple buckle, designed by Sonia Rykiel.

Noted fashion critic Matt Drudge expressed a critical opinion about her fashion risk-taking in London. "LONDON SHOCK FASHION," declared Drudge. "Michelle and the orange snake."

"Has the usually fashion-careful first lady gone too far?" he asks, repeating Gressa's question. "What are those flowery bands around her midsection?"[20]

Drudge has company. "Michelle Obama Puts Her Reputation for Style on the Line as She Sports a Garish Outfit on a Trip to Westminster Abbey," shrieked the United Kingdom's The Sun in its June 10, 2009, issue.

Michelle "was brilliant in white for D-Day, but this color extravaganza may be reaching too far to the other end of the spectrum," said Liisa O'Neill, New York Daily News staff writer, who agreed with Drudge. "Did Michelle Obama finally take a fashion misstep?" Liisa asked. "What do you think?"[21] (The present author, who admires Michelle Obama tremendously, thinks yes. In fact, she considers the outfit atrocious.)

The multitude of news stories about Michelle Obama's clothes would make you think she had been chosen for a new cabinet position, Secretary of Fashion. Yet many commentators, while appreciating Michelle's fashion sense, would prefer to see her recognized for her substance, not just for her style.

Michelle successfully complements her wardrobe, either brazenly, with fantastic faux jewels, or delightfully, with a playful brooch or a simple bow. Any first lady easily could be decked out in priceless diamonds and pearls. But Michelle chooses what she likes because she likes it, not by the price of the item. She has thrown herself into her new position as an international role model as if born to it. And however she does it, Michelle always makes her chic appearance seem effortless.

Michelle Obama is the same on the outside as she is on the inside, a modern American working mother. Her outfits appear comfortable rather than rigid, and she looks pretty instead of conventional. The sportswear she loves is also the favorite of most American women.

Warm, confident, frank and open, and possessing the uncanny ability to connect with all kinds of people, Michelle is a person everybody wants to know. And that is exactly what she looks like.[22]

Michelle shows little interest in the big names of American fashion, those who employ thousands and thousands of people and are famous all over the world. Her early choices of clothing by Jason Wu, Isabel Toledo, and Thakoon charmed people around the globe and excited a whole industry. "But with economic recovery none too close," Bridget Foley of *WWD* asks, "should she diversify her wardrobe choices? Indeed, does she have a responsibility to do so?"

Vera Wang agrees: "I love seeing young designers and their vision and how they grow," she told *WWD*. "On the other hand, of course, I wish she would consider some of us."[23]

With all the fuss over Michelle's sleeveless dresses, she is by no means the first of the first ladies to wear them. According to Carl Sferazza Anthony, first lady historian, Dolley Madison, Florence Harding, Frances Cleveland, Grace Coolidge, and even dowdy Mamie Eisenhower all wore sleeveless numbers that called forth allegations of indecency. The bared shoulders of Jackie Kennedy and Nancy Reagan, however, instigated little if any comment. It seems that when it came to her wardrobe, Jackie could get away with anything.

Michelle's clothing projects an air of authenticity, self-confidence, intelligence, glowing health, and optimism, and as such reflects the spirit of the 21st century. Something new pervades the air, the scent of youthful freedom and openness. It is evident on the streets, in the young women who flaunt their coquettish skirts with bare legs and brightly colored pocketbooks like Michelle's, and think nothing of pairing simple tank tops with elegant scarves and squeezing their tight-fitting jeans into handsome boots.[24]

Nevertheless, *WWD* demands, "Where in the world are Donna, Ralph and Calvin?" The enchanting and perhaps mischievous Michelle Obama, who dared to wear a cardigan to Buckingham Palace to meet the Queen, is not the person to ask.

Oscar De la Renta was more blunt about it than his colleagues: "You don't go to Buckingham Palace in a sweater."[25]

"Oh please," countered Gioia Diliberto in the *Huffington Post*. "Let Michelle wear what she wants."[26]

In a declaration that reveals a great deal about Michelle Obama's character, she has disclosed that she never wears furs. According to an article in the *Washington Times,* this information was made public after Carla Bruni-Sarkozy, first lady of France, stated that she does not own any furs.[27]

Michelle's public anti-fur position is a tremendous step forward for animal rights. Her stance against the murder of animals for the sake of women's fashion is a stand against animal cruelty and a further indication of Michelle Obama's kind, considerate heart.

How fitting that Michelle Obama was honored for her contributions to fashion at the industry's annual awards ceremony! In handing the prestigious award to the first lady, Diane von Furstenberg, president of the Council of Fashion Designers of America, lauded her "unique look that balances the duality of her lives in her roles as trusted adviser to her husband, President Barack Obama, and busy mother to their two daughters," and her "meteoric rise as a fashion icon."[28]

NOTES

1. Maria Puente, "Excitement Builds over Obama's Fashion Sense," *USA Today,* December 18, 2008, http://www.usatoday.com/printedition/news/20081218/1amichelle18_va.art.htm.

2. Terri Agins, "Over-40 Finds a Muse," *Wall Street Journal*, December 6, 2008, http://online.wsj.com/article/SB122852270571084377.html.

3. Bridget Foley and Bobbi Queen, "Michelle Obama: What Should She Wear?," *WWD*, December 1, 2008, http://www.wwd.com/fashion-news/dressing-the-first-lady-1875632.

4. Bonnie Fuller, "Why Michelle's Red Dress Just Shook the World," *Huffington Post*, November 11, 2008, http://www.huffingtonpost.com/bonnie-fuller/why-michelles-red-dress-j_b_143041.html.

5. Mandi Norwood, quoted in Puente, "Excitement Builds over Obama's Fashion Sense."

6. Cloe Cabrera, "Michelle to Hit D.C. in Style," *Media General News Service*, January 6, 2009, http://inauguration.mgnetwork.com/ine/news/national/national_govtpolitics/article/michelle_to_hit_d.c._in_style/2705/?site_id=WDB.

7. Ibid.

8. Ibid.

9. Ibid.

10. Lesley Jane Seymour, "Behind the *More* Magazine Shoot: Who Dictates Michelle Obama's Personal Style?," *Huffington Post*, September 22, 2008, http://www.huffingtonpost.com/lesley-jane-seymour/ dressgate-who-is-dictatin_b_128067.html.

11. Shaena Henry, "Michelle Obama: The Accidental Fashionista," *Huffington Post*, March 30, 2009, http://www.huffingtonpost.com/ shaena-henry/michelle-obama-the-accide_b_180560.html.

12. Guy Trebay, "U.S. Fashion's One-Woman Bailout?," *New York Times*, January 7, 2009, http://www.nytimes.com/2009/01/08/ style/08iht-08michelle.19181409.html.

13. Ibid.

14. "Michelle Obama's Style Admired, She's Been Compared with Jacqueline Kennedy," Austin News KXAN.com, January 18, 2009, http://www.kxan.com/dpp/news/national/Michelle_Obamas_style_ admired.

15. Stacy A. Cordery, "What About Michelle's First Hundred Days?" *History News Network*, April 26, 2009.

16. "Michelle Obama's Style Admired, She's Been Compared with Jacqueline Kennedy."

17. Catherine Moran, "US to Witness More Ethnic, Class Diversity in Michelle Obama's Fashions," *Asian News International*, January 24, 2009, http://www.thefreelibrary.com/'US+to+witness+more+ethnic,+ class+diversity+in+Michelle+Obama's...-a0212311199.

18. Jessica Gressa, "Michelle Not New Jackie Kennedy," *Badger Herald*, January 25, 2009.

19. Ibid.

20. Julie Mason, "Michelle Obama Fashion Shocker!," WashingtonExaminer.com, June 10, 2009, http://www.washingtonexaminer.com/ opinion/blogs/beltway-confidential/Michelle-Obama-fashion-shocker-47526227.html. Page no longer available.

21. Lisa O'Neill, "First Lady Michelle Obama's First Fashion Misstep, Michelle's Burst of Color," *Daily News*, June 11, 2009, http:// www.nydailynews.com/lifestyle/fashion/2009/06/11/2009-06-11_first_ lady_michelle_obamas_first_fashion_misstep_you_tell_us.html. Page no longer available.

22. Hal Rubenstein, "Michelle Obama: America's New Style Icon Knows Just What to Pack," *InStyle* magazine, April 6, 2009.

23. Bridget Foley, "Dressing Michelle: Major Designers Wait for First Lady's Call," *WWD*, April 2, 2009, http://www.wwd.com/fashion-news/major-designers-wait-for-first-ladys-call-2090453?src=bblast/040309#/article/fashion-news/major-designers-wait-for-first-ladys-call-2090453?page=1.

24. Gioia Diliberto, "Michelle Obama's New Kind of Glamour," *Huffington Post,* April 4, 2009.

25. Foley, "Dressing Michelle: Major Designers Wait for First Lady's Call."

26. Gioia Diliberto, "Why Designers Are Dissing Michelle," *Huffington Post,* April 8, 2009, http://www.huffingtonpost.com/gioia-diliberto/why-designers-are-dissing_b_183964.html.

27. Elizabeth Holli Wood, "Michelle Obama Says 'No' to Fur, What about Leather?," *Tampa Vegan Examiner,* June 12, 2009.

28. Samantha Critchell, "Fashion World Honors New Stars Rodarte and Obama," KXNet.com, June 16, 2009.

Chapter 13

MICHELLE OBAMA AMONG THE FIRST LADIES

We cannot imagine the depth and extent of any first lady's influence on her husband unless we have some written record of it, such as a letter, memoir, or published interview. We know, for example, from Jackie Kennedy's drafting of her husband's endorsement of Adlai Stevenson for president how influential she was in this respect, and even more important, in her stance against nuclear weapons. Other instances kept for posterity are Eleanor Roosevelt's note to Cabinet members containing her paralyzed husband's instructions to them; Nancy Reagan's comments about her husband's appearances, as described in Chief of Staff Don Regan's book; and military aide Benjamin Montgomery's statement that Ida McKinley's opinion was crucial in persuading her husband to retain possession of the Philippines after the Spanish–American War.[1]

Although precisely how much influence Michelle Obama has over her husband may never be known, we do know that the president has a great deal of respect for his wife and her opinions. After all, he calls her "the Boss," and is always saying, "Gotta check with the boss." It also has been said that she wears the pants in the family.

According to service advocates who asked not to be named, some decisions already are being made by the first lady. For example, they say that Michelle Obama is in the driver's seat of the Corporation for National and Community Service (CNCS), and her former chief of staff, Jackie Norris, moved to CNCS as a senior advisor.[2]

Let us examine how Michelle Obama's strengths and experience, as well as her possible weaknesses, could influence her husband's thinking.

Although Barack Obama had worked in the community, his pre–White House career was confined largely to his experiences in the legislature. In contrast to her husband, Michelle Obama has much more community experience. Her resume abounds with executive positions.

Michelle's thinking, as formed by her considerable and highly efficient executive experience, could influence her husband's decisions greatly. Profiles and interviews of Michelle Obama intimate that her advice already has played an important role at decisive moments in Barack's career. During the campaign, she was called "the closer," because she often was able to convince undecided voters to cast their ballots for Obama. As a fine public speaker whose words come from her heart, Michelle also counseled Barack to be more emotional and less cerebral in his important speeches. Unlike most people, she is not intimidated by the office of the president of the United States, and doesn't hesitate to chastise her husband if she feels he deserves it, as demonstrated by her sharply aimed digs when he fails to do his share of work around the house. Once Barack poignantly mused, "I wonder if John McCain has to carry out the garbage." It is unknown whether Michelle feels the president of the United States still has to empty the trash cans.

"Her role is whatever she thinks she can make the biggest difference [in]," Obama predicted in December 2007 of his wife as first lady, "Which isn't to say she won't be telling me what to do."[3]

Senior White House Advisor David Axelrod said in a television interview that Michelle asked Barack a meaningful and crucial question before giving her blessing to his running for president. "What do you think you can provide that the other candidates can't?"

Her directness, along with her managerial background, could prove essential in assessing the value and integrity of key personnel. For a president overloaded with work, the presence of a competent staff can be a major factor in designing and giving the go ahead to policy. Even first ladies who were not interested in policy often took an active role when they intuited a bungler in the president's coterie.

With women supposedly more intuitive than men, most presidents look to their wives for insight into character. Lincoln's actions were sometimes determined by his wife's judgments, as indicated in his statement, "I give you credit for sagacity." President Kennedy, in particular, put much credence in his wife's "shit detector" skills and often consulted her about the character of colleagues. For example, Jackie's distrust of "mad bomber" Air Force General Curtis LeMay escalated JFK's mistrust of him.[4]

Obama does not lack the advice of competent assistants, but a president often is flooded with a stream of decisions and unexpected crises. First ladies, especially if they are as gregarious as Michelle Obama, hear more uncensored talk from the West Wing and from aides, who may confide in the first lady what they hesitate to tell *the president*. As Nancy Reagan had a West Wing contact in her old friend Mike Deaver, Michelle Obama has a deep personal bond with Valerie Jarrett, her former boss at the Chicago mayor's office, who now serves as senior advisor to the president. Valerie Jarrett also served on the board of the university and its medical center with Michelle. There is no doubt that Jarrett will keep Michelle in the know about any hostility between advisors when the president is traveling or occupied with more important matters.

It is also easier for first ladies than for their husbands to make contact with the world outside the White House. Eleanor Roosevelt perfected the role of informant to her husband and served as Roosevelt's legs when his paralysis kept him from moving easily around New York State as its governor. She was even more useful during his presidential terms in helping him to tour areas devastated by the Depression. She also appeared without notice in improbable places, where she got people to speak with her in depth about their problems, so she could judge whether FDR's New Deal programs were helping to resolve them.

Michelle Obama, like Mrs. Roosevelt more than half a century ago, enjoys coming into direct contact with people and speaking with them, without walls erected between them.

When Michelle Obama heard of the acute difficulties experienced by military families, she sought ways to improve them, no doubt with the president's backing. We have every reason to believe that Michelle shares her findings, be they large or small, with her husband.

Eleanor Roosevelt was known for presenting a variety of disparate voices to her husband, thus widening and deepening his perspective on his constituents. Michelle Obama has demonstrated similar talents, in that she has created diverse committees and advisory boards for organizations she has headed. Although Obama himself is superb at seeking out diversity in government officials, Michelle's continued input can considerably widen their personal contacts when he is occupied with urgent government business.[5]

Nancy Reagan greatly expanded her husband's thinking during the Iran-Contra affair, when she introduced him to Bob Strauss, the former Democratic National Chairman. Nancy also had a hand in the dismissal of Don Regan, her husband's chief of staff. She said he was "really a terrible man," and asked Bob Strauss to help her convince the president that her opinion was justified. She said Regan once hung up on her during a phone conversation. "When Ronnie found out about that, that did it," she said.

When lauded for being a wonderful wife, Nancy Reagan said she was just doing what any caring spouse would do to help her husband conduct his business. While the public is most aware of Mrs. Reagan's drug-abuse project ("Just say no to drugs"), her impact on Ronald Reagan was even greater as his loving wife.

Speaking of Nancy Reagan, it is interesting that Michelle called her for advice on how to run the White House. In response, Nancy suggested that the Obamas follow the Reagans' example and hold many state dinners. The Reagans hosted 56 of them, in contrast to the meager 6 held by President George W. Bush and Laura Bush. "Just have a good time and do a little business. And that is the way Washington works," Nancy said to the present first lady.[6]

The White House confirmed that Michelle had telephoned Nancy Reagan at least once, when the two women had a conversation of

45 minutes. "She called me for advice, suggestions; I was very happy to talk to her," Reagan said in an interview with *Vanity Fair* magazine. "We had a nice conversation."[7]

Betty Ford spoke of her influence on her husband as "pillow talk," while Pat Nixon, in terms later echoed by Nancy Reagan, said she was simply being a "helpmeet."[8]

Many former first ladies are close to each other. Laura Bush told Robin Roberts in an interview with *Good Morning America* that former first ladies are "sort of like a club. Everybody who's been there before knows what the new person is discovering."[9]

Rosalynn Carter is another first lady who has spoken with Michelle on many subjects since Obama was inaugurated. According to a spokeswoman, Carter has given the same advice to all the first ladies who followed her, "Select a few key projects, stand by your convictions, and ignore the criticisms."[10] From what we know about Michelle Obama, she should have no difficulty in following Carter's advice.

Michelle Obama appreciates the advice of her forebears, and told *Time* magazine, "I think there's a real camaraderie among first ladies that I sense, just the willingness and openness of each and every one of them, just the sense of, 'I know what you're about to go through and I'm with you.'"[11]

To our knowledge, no first lady has succeeded in getting a president to approve a policy simply because she wanted it passed: presidential wives must present their husbands with as solid a case for their pet issues as any official or cabinet member. John F. Kennedy had to be convinced that his wife knew what she was doing in her restoration of the White House before he would ask Congress to pass a bill allotting funds for the project.

While Jacqueline Kennedy was admired for her historically accurate redecoration and preservation of the White House, it is generally unknown that Lucretia Garfield began such a restoration long before Jackie, only to be cut short six months after her husband James Garfield's inauguration in 1881 when he was assassinated. It is interesting, too, that both women won respect for their strength and courage after their husbands were assassinated.

Following the examples set by great first ladies before her, it is very possible that Michelle Obama will seek an affiliation with Tom

Daschle, director of the White House Office of Health Care Reform, to help in her quest to assist working mothers. Michelle also may form an alliance with Barack Obama's veterans affairs secretary, retired General Eric Shinseki, to render support to military families.

Fortunately, Michelle Obama, in overcoming the sudden strangeness of her life, will have easy access to the Secretary of State in the White House. In 1992, Hillary Rodham Clinton spoke of the trials of a first lady when she declared, "Our lives are a mixture of different roles. Most of us are doing the best we can to find whatever the right balance is. For me, that balance is family, work and service." We do not know what difficulties Michelle Obama will have to face in her tenure as first lady, but trust that she will handle whatever they may be with strength and dignity. We hope she will not have to say, as did Jacqueline Kennedy, "I think my biggest achievement is that after going through a rather difficult time, I consider myself comparatively sane."[12]

In contrast to Hillary Clinton, who loathed being first lady, and Laura Bush, who played the role of little wife, Michelle, Maureen Dowd informs us, "has soared every day, expanding the job to show us what can be accomplished by a generous spirit, a confident nature and a well-disciplined body."[13] Unlike her immediate predecessors, it seems, Michelle Obama was made for the job of first lady, and the job was made for her.

Michelle Obama may well turn out to have the greatest impact of any first lady in history during the course of her husband's presidency. Besides being remarkably experienced in community work, Michelle is deeply loved and respected by Barack. The words of a loved one have a greater impact than the conversation of a stranger. In addition, she was Barack's mentor and adviser. Some of that relationship must have stuck, even though his station is now beyond hers. Such conferences belong in what Hillary Clinton named a "zone of privacy" and serve to keep a first lady above criticism. Therefore, we can only speculate on how much influence Michelle Obama has and will have on the president and the running of the country.

Michelle says she is not interested in politics. "If politics were my passion," she informed a *Chicago Tribune* reporter, "I'd find out how to do it and make it work." Her family is her passion, and, indeed, she makes it work. And advising the president is part of her passion.[14]

The official portrait of First Lady Michelle Obama. Photograph by Joyce N. Boghosian. (Library of Congress.)

In addition to their love for each other and their daughters, the Obamas share a calling to perform community service. It is well known that Michelle first fell in love with Barack when she heard him speak at a community meeting, and that a similar interest pulled the graduate of Harvard Law School back to the neighborhood where she was born. It is also common knowledge that their mutual passion for social welfare asserted itself again when she left a prestigious Chicago law firm to join Public Allies, at a significant loss of salary.

Presidential couples are often bound together by an interest they share. The Reagans were fellow actors, the Clintons were lawyers. Herbert and Lou Hoover were geology students at Stanford University who translated an ancient mineralogy text together. And, of course, community service binds the Obamas together. As a result, they volunteered together before the inauguration on a National Day of Service, in place of the usual series of events that traditionally welcome the first lady. In all likelihood, Michelle will continue the Renew America Together project that is so dear to the hearts of both the Obamas.[15]

But, of the many ways Michelle Obama can influence the president, the most important is through the power of her love and support, which is evident when one sees the adoration and admiration
in the president's eyes for the love of his life. One can almost see Michelle's strength pouring into him. It is as if together they make up
the presidency. The world is not aware of the important role played
by many first ladies in the election of their husbands, many of whom
never would have become president without the help of their wives.
For example, Martha Washington's immense wealth enabled George to
enter and remain in politics, Lincoln had no social or political entrée
without his wife Mary's powerful family connections, and Taft never
could have run for the presidency at all if not for the administrative
ability of Nellie, his wife.[16]

Like Washington, Lincoln, and Taft, Barack Obama could not have
been elected president on his own. Imagine what the presidential
campaign would have looked like without the presence of Michelle.
According to British commentator Gaby Wood, Michelle Obama is
not content to merely sit back and let her husband take center stage—
indeed, she is responsible for drastically changing Barack Obama's
public image. During her husband's campaign, she played the perfect
counterpart. She discussed her children and teased her husband in
public, making him seem much more accessible. The stories about her
background humanized her husband and made him seem much more
all-American than his foreign upbringing and Ivy League education
could have done on its own. She didn't just support her husband's campaign, she helped create it.[17]

The dramatic assistance given their husbands often requires sacrifices of the part of presidential wives. Although most first ladies before
Hillary Clinton had no professional careers to renounce, all had to give
up their privacy, and some even forfeited their mental and physical
health. Many were cheated of a wished-for retirement with their husbands. Peggy Taylor said her husband's nomination was a plot to de-
prive her of his society and shorten his life. Sadly enough, she turned
out to be right: he died after holding office for only 16 months. Pat
Nixon said her husband's presidency cost her "everything I ever cared
about." Other presidential wives, such as Bess Truman, Louisa Adams,
and Eleanor Roosevelt, suffered estrangement from their husbands

under the stress of their office.[18] Mamie Eisenhower turned to alcohol and Betty Ford to drugs for relief. Worst of all, the assassination of President Kennedy ruined the life of his wife.

Thus far in the Obama presidency, the marriage of Barack and Michelle seems to be withstanding any call for sacrifice on Michelle's part. She differs from most first ladies in several respects. In addition to the strength given her by her loving union with Barack, the role of first lady seems to have been created for Michelle, who appears happy and confident in all her public activities. As her mother gave up her job to care for Michelle and Craig when they were little, it must seem to Michelle the normal thing to do. Since she sees her major role as "Mom-in-Chief," setting her professional career aside at least temporarily does not appear to be much of a deprivation for her.

Evidently, however, Michelle Obama is not always quite as self-confident as she looks. She told the graduating class of a D.C. public charter school that, like the rest of us, she and the president still entertain doubts about their abilities, but they look past such worries, and so should the students.

"We all had doubts," she said. "We all heard nagging voices, sometimes we still do, asking us, 'Will we be able to compete in this new arena? But in the end, we were all more than ready. . . . I was more than ready, and Barack Obama certainly is more than ready."[19]

Michelle is widely known for her frankness and lack of interest in what people think of her. When the press first began to buzz around Barack like bees around honey, Michelle wryly suggested that they wait and see what he accomplished before heaping so much praise on him. Intimating that he doesn't walk on water, she kept his admirers (and him) in touch with reality as she stressed that he is merely a human being.

Obama doesn't seem to mind much that his wife keeps his feet on the ground. In an interview with the Russian media giant *ITAR-TASS/ROSSIYA TV*, Obama was asked what the role of the first lady is. He answered that Michelle Obama's "first role is to make sure that our children are doing well" and her "second job is to make sure that I don't get too cocky." Michelle "reminds me of all the things that I can improve on," the president said.[20]

Obama is seen by the public as calm and cool under pressure. That may be, but one must wonder why he finds it necessary to be a smoker, even though his wife exacted a promise before he ran for president that he would give up the habit if she backed him in the campaign. She said, "To me it's a role model thing. You can smoke or you can be President." She kept her promise: he didn't, or hasn't as yet.

Obama is not the only president to have broken a promise to his wife. After Richard Nixon was defeated in the race for governor of California in 1962, he promised Pat that he was finished with politics. He would have lost the 1968 election had he not broken that pledge. It was only after Pat died that Nixon was able to reveal how dependent he had been on the wife experts usually dismiss as insignificant to his career.

Richard Nixon was asked before he left the White House in disgrace how he was able to rant on and on about his saintly mother and mention the gratitude he felt to his faithful aides and domestic staff without acknowledging the contributions of the wife standing obediently behind him. He answered that his need for her was so monumental that had he spoken of it he would have cracked up. Nineteen years later, he proved that his fears had been justified. At Pat's funeral in 1993, he did just that. Sobbing openly, he became the epitome of a broken down man who now was truly alone.[21]

In contrast, six minutes after Barack Obama began his victory speech in 2008, he attested to the "unyielding support of my best friend for the last sixteen years, the rock of our family and the love of my life." Such is the measure of the two men.

"The first lady has always been the approachable public face of the presidential administration. While a president is concentrating on business, the first lady almost by definition is the one there to show compassion," according to Lisa Kathleen Graddy, curator of the First Ladies Collection at the Smithsonian's Museum of American History. "Some call it the white-glove pulpit."

"When George Washington was president," Graddy said, "veterans who could not see the president would come to the door and talk to Mrs. Washington. The first lady is a public advocate. But she is the official female figure representing our country in a ceremonial way."[22]

Michelle Obama has said she will concentrate on issues concerning the balance of work and family, problems of military families, and community service. One of her aides put it well when she said,

"Mrs. Obama will define the role of first lady for herself—blending family and issues of great importance to her. Nancy Reagan said years ago, 'The Constitution doesn't mention the president's wife. Each incoming first lady has had to define the job herself.' Mrs. Obama will do the same."

Jacqueline Kennedy renovated the White House. Lady Bird Johnson worked on beautification. Nancy Reagan was the advocate of "just say no" to drugs. Laura Bush's interest was the spread of literacy. "Eleanor Roosevelt didn't have one project," said Myra G. Gutin, a first lady historian and author of *The President's Partner: The First Lady in the Twentieth Century*. "She was all over the board. She was involved in New Deal programs. She was active in policy. . . . But," Gutin continued, "I don't think it is right to say Michelle Obama will be the next Eleanor Roosevelt."[23]

Not every expert agrees with Gutin. For example, Nathan Richter, managing director at Wakefield, a survey research and communications consultancy, believes that Michelle Obama most resembles the great American icon Eleanor Roosevelt, who said, "Every woman in public life needs to develop skin as tough as rhinoceros hide."[24]

Mrs. Roosevelt was constantly attacked during her 12 years as first lady, as much because she was as great a star as her husband as for her policies. Earlier first ladies who also were routinely criticized include Louisa Adams, who was born in England, and her husband John Quincy Adams, who were assaulted without basis by ignoramuses for being lovers of royalty who supposedly encouraged a sexual relationship between the czar and one of Louisa's aides. The campaign between Adams and Andrew Jackson in 1828 was the first to include a barrage against a candidate's wife. The spunky Louisa was the first presidential spouse to fight back, giving a rebuttal in a widely read women's magazine.[25]

More recently, Rosalynn Carter was mocked for not serving hard liquor in the White House, but Lucy Hayes, wife of Rutherford B. Hayes, and Sarah Polk, wife of James Polk, banned all drinking, dancing, and card playing in the White House long before Carter became first lady.

Nancy Reagan's routine consultations with an astrologer to help plan her husband's schedules were greeted with derision, but she was not alone in seeking help from the heavens. Florence Harding, wife of Warren G. Harding, also sought celestial help in 1920, and Mary Todd Lincoln was known to hold actual séances in the White House.[26]

Michelle Obama already has received more than her share of battering by the media. When president-elect Obama publicly thanked Michelle for her contribution to his winning the election in his presidential victory speech, it must have soothed the racist wounds inflicted on her during the campaign by *Fox News*, who had sullied her with the nasty title of "Obama's baby mama" and called the fist-bump between the Obamas a "terrorist fist jab." Yet Michelle remained astonishingly untouched by the hateful charges and, exhibiting grace under fire, ignored the savage verbal attacks and continued to campaign for her husband as efficiently as ever.[27] The strength she demonstrated during the campaign proves that Michelle Obama undoubtedly meets Eleanor Roosevelt's standard for women in public life—that she develop "skin as tough as rhinoceros hide."

Michelle shares other characteristics with Eleanor Roosevelt besides a "tough hide": an unflappable manner, brilliance, originality, and rejection of the traditional role of first lady.

Michelle, like her husband, is a talented public speaker whose speeches are moving as well as amusing. Her obvious sincerity and commitment to issues she believes in awaken an overwhelming reaction of trust and admiration in crowd after crowd. Michelle, in common with Mrs. Roosevelt, is a charismatic woman who connects with Americans of all classes and creeds. In a pleasant contrast to Barack's rock-star popularity, Michelle is firmly rooted on the ground.

Michelle's charm became visible to the public as soon as Barack Obama was sworn in. Demonstrating their intention of "walking the walk, as well as talking the talk," both Obamas danced with military personnel at the Armed Forces Ball, illustrating Michelle's goal as first lady of improving the lives of armed services members and families.[28]

This mutual interest in the military is another quality shared by Michelle and Mrs. Roosevelt, who spent a great deal of time visiting servicemen during World War II. With their similarity in character and interests, Michelle Obama may well leave the White House having earned the level of respect gained by Eleanor Roosevelt over a half century ago.

A few questions about Michelle Obama as first lady still linger. Which first lady or ladies will she resemble the most? Will she be a second Hillary Clinton, in which the country will get "two for the price of one"? I personally believe that Michelle Obama will surpass Hillary Clinton as our most influential first lady, and then some.

Some of Jackie Kennedy's style and grace shine through Michelle's poised appearances. Despite Gutin's belief that it is unfair to say Michelle Obama will be another Eleanor Roosevelt, the present first lady seems to have Mrs. Roosevelt's political astuteness and compassion for people of every race and gender. Nevertheless, even though Michelle shares many of the qualities of the great first ladies of the past, she is a unique individual. Although she has given broad hints as to the issues she will pursue, nobody as yet can say for sure.

What kind of record will Michelle Obama leave in the annals of history? I suspect she will be one of a kind, and that her brilliance, charm, integrity, philosophy of life, and goodness of heart will leave a mark upon the United States that will equal and possibly even surpass that of every former first lady. But, regardless of what history may have to say about Michelle Obama, with her great joy in being first lady, there is no doubt she is a winner. As Shakespeare said, "Things won are done, joy's soul lies in the doing."

Unlike Michelle Obama, Martha Washington, the first first lady, found her role imprisoning, "I think I am more like a state prisoner than anything else," she wrote, "there is certain bonds set for me which I must not depart from." Despite her awareness that she occupied a special place in history that "many younger and gayer women would be extremely pleased in my place," she would very much have preferred to remain at home.[29]

First Lady Jacqueline Kennedy also did not care for the job. She said, "The one thing I do not want to be called is 'first lady.' It sounds like a saddle horse."[30] Michelle Obama calls herself "Mom-in-Chief," placing her ideals before the public from the beginning. Jackie Kennedy and Michelle Obama are alike in that both regard family values above all others.

Lady Bird Johnson, of whom Jacqueline Kennedy said, "She would have crawled down Pennsylvania Avenue on her knees upon glass for Lyndon," said, in an uncharacteristic moment, "A politician ought to be born a foundling and remain a bachelor."[31] Like Jacqueline Kennedy, Pat Nixon intensely disliked the role of first lady. Both Peggy Taylor and Eliza Johnson appointed their daughters to host in their place. Despite her dislike of haute couture, Eleanor Roosevelt suffered uncomfortable hats and clothing in her many appearances in place of her ill husband. Mrs. Roosevelt valiantly overcame paralyzing timidity and self-doubts about her lack of beauty and style, and learned to charm audiences with her warmth and grace under pressure. She eventually was able to conclude that "no matter how plain a woman may be, if truth and loyalty are stamped upon her face, all will be attracted to her."[32] The courageous Mrs. Roosevelt braved the currents of the day to become the first white resident of Washington D.C. to join the National Association for the Advancement of Colored People. There may be many more first ladies (as well as presidents) who disliked their jobs, but they were more close-mouthed about it than these ladies, and we will never know their secrets.

NOTES

1. Carl Sferrazza Anthony, "Michelle Obama and the Covert Influence of First Ladies," *Huffington Post*, January 30, 2009, http://www.huffingtonpost.com/carl-sferrazza-anthony/michelle-obama-and-the-co_b_162548.html.

2. Robin Givhan, "First Lady Replaces Her Chief of Staff," *Washington Post*, June 5, 2009, http://www.washingtonpost.com/wp-dyn/content/article/2009/06/04/AR2009060404285.html.

3. Anthony, "Michelle Obama and the Covert Influence of First Ladies."

4. Alma H. Bond, *Jackie O on the Couch*, in publication.

5. Anthony, "Michelle Obama and the Covert Influence of First Ladies."

6. Bob Colacello, "Nancy Reagan's Solo Role," *Vanity Fair*, June 1, 2009, http://www.vanityfair.com/politics/features/2009/07/nancy-reagan200907.

7. Ibid.

8. Anthony, "Michelle Obama and the Covert Influence of First Ladies."

9. Robin Roberts, interview with Laura Bush, *Good Morning America*; quoted in Kate Snow, "Former First Ladies Counsel Michelle Obama to Make Camp David a Priority, With Open Arms and Plenty of Advice, N. Reagan and L. Bush Welcome M. Obama to the First Ladies Club," *ABC News*, June 4, 2009.

10. Ibid.

11. Michael Scherer and Nancy Gibbs, "Interview with the First Lady," *Time* magazine, May 21, 2009, http://www.time.com/time/politics/article/0,8599,1899741-4,00.html. Page no longer available.

12. Nathan Richter, "Michelle Obama and the Third Roosevelt," *Globalist*, March 10, 2009.

13. Maureen Dowd, "Should Michelle Cover Up?" *New York Times*, March 7, 2009, http://www.nytimes.com/2009/03/08/opinion/08dowd.html.

14. Anthony, "Michelle Obama and the Covert Influence of First Ladies."

15. Ibid.

16. Gaby Wood, "The Observer: Yes, Michelle Obama Can, First Lady, Mom-in-Chief, Role Model, Fashion Icon, Dinner Lady, Serial Hugger; Twelve Top Female Writers Celebrate the Many Faces of Michelle Obama," Guardian.co.uk, May 3, 2009.

17. Ibid.

18. Anthony, "Michelle Obama and the Covert Influence of First Ladies."

19. Jon Ward, "First Lady Rallies Grads," *Washington Times*, June 4, 2009.

20. Jake Tapper, "Asked What He Doesn't Like about Himself, President Obama Cites His Golf Game," *ABC News*, July 5, 2009.

21. Anthony, "Michelle Obama and the Covert Influence of First Ladies."

22. Lisa Kathleen Graddy, quoted in DeNeen L. Brown, "Michelle Obama Will Define Her First-Lady Role as She Goes," *Washington Post*, January 20, 2009, http://www.washingtonpost.com/wp-dyn/content/article/2009/01/19/AR2009011903139.html?sid=ST2009012000026.

23. Myra Gutin, ibid.

24. Richter, "Michelle Obama and the Third Roosevelt."

25. Maria Puente, "First Ladies: Drawing Some Parallels," *USA Today,* October 21, 2008, http://www.usatoday.com/life/people/2008-10-21-first-ladies-side_N.htm. Page no longer available.

26. Ibid.

27. Richter, "Michelle Obama and the Third Roosevelt."

28. Ibid.

29. "Martha Dandridge Custis Washington," The White House, undated, http://www.whitehouse.gov/about/liveproduction/martha-dandridge-custis-washington.

30. J. E. Lighter, "Taking Notice of POTUS," *Atlantic Monthly,* October 1997, http://www.theatlantic.com/past/docs/issues/97oct/wordimp.htm.

31. Lady Bird, "Three First Ladies at Big Arts," http://www.tea for three.com/reviews.html. Page no longer available.

32. "Anna Eleanor Roosevelt," The White House, undated, http://www.whitehouse.gov/about/first-ladies/eleanorroosevelt.

SELECTED BIBLIOGRAPHY

BOOKS AND BOOK-LENGTH WORKS

Bergen Brophy, David. *Michelle Obama: Meet the First Lady*. New York: HarperCollins, 2009.

The story of the South Side girl who has inspired our nation to believe in the American dream exemplified by her life.

Bond, Alma H. *Jackie O: On the Couch*. Baltimore, MD: Bancroft Press, 2011.

Colbert, David. *Michele Obama: An American Story*. Boston and New York: Sandpiper, Houghton Mifflin Harcourt, 2009.

The story of Michelle Obama's life, as she carves out a new chapter in history that is old-fashioned in many ways as well as natural and genuine.

Horton, James Oliver, and Lois E. Horton. *Slavery and the Making of America*. New York: Oxford University Press, 2005.

Africans and African Americans appear not just as "passive laborers" but as shapers of American culture, from colonial politics to Southern cuisine.

Jones, Susan A., ed. *Michelle Obama: In Her Own Words*. New York: PublicAffairs, 2009.

The speeches given by Michelle Obama that may have helped win her husband the presidency, including her address to the National Democratic Convention.

Lightfoot, Elizabeth. *Michelle Obama, First Lady of Hope*. Guilford, CT: Lyons Press, 2009.

The astonishing tale of a woman whose character and intellect in all likelihood will make her one of the most influential first ladies in history.

Mundy, Liza. *Michelle: A Biography*. New York: Simon and Schuster, 2008.

The first and, as of this writing, the best of the published biographies of Michelle Obama.

Norwood, Mandi. *Michelle Style*. New York: William Morrow, 2009.

This one-of-a-kind volume spotlights and celebrates our remarkable 21st-century icon of fashion.

Obama, Barack. *The Audacity of Hope*. New York: Three Rivers Press, an imprint of Crown Publishing Group, Random House, 2006.

Movingly written, Obama's first book describes his political convictions and provides humane, sensible solutions.

Obama, Barack. *Dreams from My Father*. New York: Three Rivers Press, an imprint of Crown Publishing Group, Random House, 1995.

Barack Obama's second book, a powerful voyage of self-discovery, investigates the serious questions of identity, class, and race.

Robinson, Michelle LaVaughn. "Princeton-Educated Blacks and the Black Community." Undergraduate thesis, Princeton University, 1985.

Royko, Mike. *Boss: Richard Daley of Chicago*. New York: A Plume Book, 1971.

A superb biography of Mayor Richard J. Daley and his corrupt Chicago regime.

Wilkerson, Isabel. *The Warmth of Other Suns; The Epic Story of America's Great Migration*. New York: Random House, 2010.

Sweeping account of the huge demographic shift that carried six million African Americans to the North and West beginning in the early 20th century, anchored in the stories of three

African Americans raised in the Jim Crow South who fled to new lives in Milwaukee, New York City, and California.

ARTICLES

Adams, Janus. "To Michelle Obama, and Her Sister 'First Ladies.'" *Women's Media Center*, March 1, 2009, reposted at: http://www.opednews.com/articles/To-Michelle-Obama-and-Her-by-Janus-Adams-090228-641.html. Page no longer available.

Anthony, Carl Sferrazza. "Michelle Obama and the Covert Influence of First Ladies." *Huffington Post*, January 30, 2009.

Antonowicz, Anton. "Michelle Obama: Trace Her Amazing Journey from Slave Street to the White House, Mirror.co.uk, December 7, 2009, http://www.mirror.co.uk/news/top-stories/2009/01/19/michelle-obama-trace-her-amazing-journey-from-slave-street-to-the-white-house-115875-21052273/. Page no longer available.

Austin News, "Michelle Obama's Style Admired; She's Been Compared with Jacqueline Kennedy." KXAN.com, January 18, 2009, http://www.kxan.com/dpp/news/national/Michelle_Obamas_style_admired.

Blake, John. "Why Michelle Obama Inspires Women around the Globe." CNN.com, April 28, 2009, http://articles.cnn.com/2009-04-28/politics/first.lady_1_first-lady-michelle-obama-women-activists?_s=PM:POLITICS. Page no longer available.

Clark, Stephen. "First 100 Days: Michelle Obama Has Big Shoes to Fill, But So Far Is Walking in Stride." *FOX News*, April 28, 2009, http://www.firstladies.org/documents/art_first100.pdf.

Colacello, Bob. "Nancy Reagan Speaks Out about Obamas, the Bushes, and Her Husband." *Vanity Fair*, June 1, 2009, http://www.vanityfair.com/online/daily/2009/06/nancy-reagan-speaks-out-about-obamas-the-bushes-and-her-husband.html. A Preview.

Collins, Lauren. "The Other Obama." *The New Yorker*, March 10, 2008, http://www.newyorker.com/reporting/2008/03/10/080310fa_fact_collins.

Cook, Mariana. "A Couple in Chicago," interview and photography session conducted in May 1996; excerpts. *The New Yorker*, January 19,

2009, http://www.newyorker.com/reporting/2009/01/19/090119fa_fact_cook.

Critchell, Samantha. "Fashion World Honors New Stars Rodarte and Obama." *Associated Press,* June 16, 2009, http://seattletimes.nwsource.com/html/entertainment/2009343799_apusfeafashioncfdaawards.html.

Dowd, Maureen. "She's Not Buttering Him Up." *The New York Times,* April 25, 2007, http://query.nytimes.com/gst/fullpage.html?res=9C05EFD9143EF936A15757C0A9619C8B63. Page no longer available.

Elisberg, Robert J. "Michelle Obama and the Hug. No, the Other Hug." *Huffington Post,* April 14, 2009, http://www.huffingtonpost.com/robert-j-elisberg/michelle-obama-and-the-hu_b_186634.html.

Glanton, Dahleen. "Pressure on Obama Daughters to Be Role Models," Chicago Tribune.com, January 14, 2009, http://www.chicagotribune.com/news/nationworld/chi-090114-obama-daughters,0,7571475.story.

Glanton, Dahleen, and Stacy St. Clair. "Fraser Robinson's Story; Michelle Obama's Family: From Slavery to White House." *Chicago Tribune,* December 4, 2008.

Gressa, Jessica. "Michelle Not New Jackie Kennedy." *The Badger Herald,* January 25, 2009, http://badgerherald.com/artsetc/2009/01/25/michelle_obama_not_n.php.

Helman, Scott. "Holding Down the Obama Family Fort, 'Grandma' Makes the Race Possible." *Boston Globe,* March 30, 2008, http://www.boston.com/news/nation/articles/2008/03/30/holding_down_the_obama_family_fort/.

Henneberger, Melinda. "The Obama Marriage; How Does It Work for Michelle Obama?" *Slate,* October 26, 2007, http://www.slate.com/id/2176683/. First Mates series, first installment.

Levinson, Molly. "Michelle: Barack's Bitter or Better Half?" *BBC News,* June 24, 2008, http://news.bbc.co.uk/2/hi/americas/7470764.stm.

Norment, Lynn. "The Hottest Couple in America." *Ebony,* February 2007, http://findarticles.com/p/articles/mi_m1077/is_4_62/ai_n27115680/.

Puente, Maria. "All Eyes and Cameras Follow First Lady to Europe." *USA Today,* March 31, 2009, http://www.usatoday.com/life/people/2009-03-30-michelle-obama-europe_N.htm. Page no longer available.

Richter, Nathan. "Michelle Obama and the Third Roosevelt." *The Globalist*, March 10, 2009, http://www.theglobalist.com/storyid.aspx?StoryId=7588. Page no longer available.

Rossi, Rosalind. "The Woman behind Obama." *Chicago Sun-Times*, January 20, 2007, http://www.suntimes.com/news/metro/221458,CST-NWS-mich21.article. Page no longer available.

Snow, Kate. "Former First Ladies Counsel Michelle Obama to Make Camp David a Priority, With Open Arms and Plenty of Advice; N. Reagan and L. Bush Welcome M. Obama to the First Ladies Club." *ABC News*, June 4, 2009, http://abcnews.go.com/Politics/story?id=7744024&page=1.

Sweet, Lynn. "Michelle Obama's 100 Days: Nearly Flawless." Chicago Sun Times.com, April 29, 2009, http://blogs.suntimes.com/sweet/2009/04/michelle_obamas_100_days_nearl.html.

Talley, André Leon. "Leading Lady." Vogue.com, March 2009, http://www.vogue.com/magazine/article/michelle-obama-leading-lady/.

Trebay, Guy. "U.S. Fashion's One-Woman Bailout?" *New York Times*, January 7, 2009, http://www.nytimes.com/2009/01/08/fashion/08michelle.html.

Walsh, Kenneth T. "Michelle Obama Makes Military Families Her Mission." *U.S. News and World Report*, March 26, 2009, http://politics.usnews.com/news/obama/articles/2009/03/26/michelle-obama-makes-military-families-her-mission.html.

Whatley, Stuart. "Obama's Daughter on Inaugural Speech." *Huffington Post*, January 16, 2009, http://www.huffingtonpost.com/2009/01/16/obamas-daughter-on-inaugu_n_158476.html.

Winfrey, Oprah. "Oprah Talks to Michelle Obama." *O Magazine*, April 2009, http://www.oprah.com/omagazine/Michelle-Obamas-Oprah-Interview-O-Magazine-Cover-with-Obama.

Wolffe, Richard. "Barack's Rock." *Newsweek*, August 28, 2007, http://www.newsweek.com/2008/02/16/barack-s-rock.html.

INDEX

About the Author

DR. ALMA HALBERT BOND is a psychoanalyst and the author of 20 published books.